Would I *Like* Jesus?

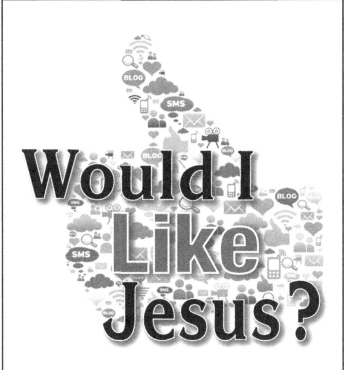

Would I Like Jesus?

A Casual Walk through the Life of Jesus

Peter Fleming

Paulist Press
New York / Mahwah, NJ

Cover image by Bildagentur Zoonar GmbH / Shutterstock.com
Cover design by Christina Cancel
Book design by Lynn Else

Library of Congress Cataloging-in-Publication Data

Fleming, Peter, 1961-
    Would I like Jesus? : a casual walk through the life of Jesus / Peter Fleming.
        pages cm
    ISBN 978-0-8091-4915-5 (pbk. : alk. paper) — ISBN 978-1-58768-478-4 (ebook)
    1. Jesus Christ—Biography. 2. Bible. Matthew—Criticism, interpretation, etc. 3. Apologetics. I. Title.
    BT301.3.F567 2015
    232.9`03—dc23

                                                                2014034146

ISBN 978-0-8091-4915-5 (paperback)
ISBN 978-1-58768-478-4 (e-book)

Published by Paulist Press
997 Macarthur Boulevard
Mahwah, New Jersey 07430

www.paulistpress.com

Printed and bound in the
United States of America

To the memory of Tom O'Donovan, S.J.
The ever faithful servant

CONTENTS

Preface..ix

Prologue xi

1. An Act of Love—Not His 1

2. New Man on the Block...5

3. The Big One...11

4. More of the Big One 17

5. The Rule Breaker...27

5½. Who Is Excluded? 42

6. The Kingdom of Heaven Is Like… 46

7. The Human Side of Jesus..48

8. Jesus and Children 52

9. Forgiving Seventy Times Seven..56

10. The Last and the First 60

11. A Few Things about Marriage...65

12. The Greatest Commandment 72

13. Going for the Jugular...75

14. Politics and Religion..80

15. The Dislikable Jesus...89

16. What Would Jesus' Students Be Like?.................................95

Epilogue...102

PREFACE

REASONS NOT TO READ THIS BOOK

1. The world is a place of limited resources, governed by fundamental natural laws of entropy and ultimate decay. We're all fighting over what little remains, and that's all there is to life.
2. Pain and suffering prove that there is no Christian God.
3. The universe can be explained as an accident. Not an accident like a car crash; just a circumstantial event, which could have been different chemically and physically and, give or take a gaseous element or two, we wouldn't have existed. So we're just an accident of an accident, nothing to get excited about, and Shakespeare and Beethoven were slumming it.
4. Since we're an accident, our thinking will always be limited to the ceiling the universe places on it; we strain to make out how we got here, we know a few things, but we can never know it all, and even if we did, it would only be to know that we're an accident limited by a ceiling… you get the idea, our thinking is forever trapped in a vicious circle.
5. There is no forever, so that last sentence is nonsense.
6. The world is nonsense.
7. It is "sound and fury, signifying nothing." (Thank you, Macbeth.)
8. It is "a tale told by an idiot." (Thank you, Shakespeare.)

9. Humanity is a nasty piece of work, for whom tribal loyalty is the greatest virtue we can achieve, and all our altruism can be psychologized away as variations on such.
10. The best thing we can do in this accidental prison of life is to distract ourselves from thinking about the inevitable annihilation awaiting us; *American Idol* is on, so you may as well watch it.

REASONS TO READ THIS BOOK

1. You want to know if life means more than an idiot's tale.
2. You want to know if life has a meaning beyond its own internal joys and woes; in other words, can the ultimate ceiling be broken?
3. You hate church people, you loathe Christians, but you wonder if Jesus Christ was better than his people.
4. You actually believe all the "Reasons Not to Read This Book," namely the idea that everything we do is meaningless, and because of that, you don't have anything better to do, and you don't much like *American Idol*.

THE REASON WHY THIS BOOK IS IRRELEVANT

If Jesus Christ is God, what does it matter if I like him or not? God is God, and has to be taken on his own terms. If God is "truth," then "truth" would be stronger than my feelings about it.

THE REASON WHY THIS BOOK IS RELEVANT

Relevant to what? To life? What does that mean? However, it's possible that there is a God, and God may be relevant to us. We may be relevant to him, unless he's one of those gods that creates a world, then leaves it and goes fishing.

PROLOGUE

Da-Da-daaaaaaaa!

Sorry. Somehow the word *prologue* makes me want dramatic opening chords. It makes me feel something important is about to be revealed, as in those movies that create whole mythological worlds and want to introduce us to the mysterious origins of their central messianic character before launching us into the story proper. I see dark clouds, lightning, mountains, perhaps a gothic spaceship swooping down to a little village, wherein lives the lowly maiden, who shall give birth to….

No?

Oh well. My love of movies and theatre will probably keep turning up like this throughout this little tome, so it's best to get used to it early—if you can stand it! (If not, shut the book. Go on! Get away before it's too late!)

Um, let's try a different tack.

For a long time, the media in the country where I live, Australia, have written about Prince Charles of England as if he were a clown, a goose, a nincompoop. Australian media tend to be dominated by Republicans—people who would like to see the end of Australia's allegiance to the British crown, which will one day be worn by Charles III.

Once when Charles came on a royal tour, he visited the headquarters of the Flying Doctor Service, the burn unit of a Perth hospital, which had saved the lives of the victims of the 2002 Bali bombings, and a research establishment in the outback, which was dedicated to developing domestic technology for far-flung indigenous communities that lacked sophisticated sewage and electrical supply. One newspaper chose to summarize this noble set of rounds with a photograph of Charles sticking his head out of an outdoor dunny (a toilet—a "john," for those dear readers who may be of an American persuasion), which had been developed at that research center. Despite the thoughtfulness he had shown to those worthy institutions, the newspaper still managed to reduce him to a silly goose! Whatever one may think of monarchy versus republic, I never believed that Charles himself was anything like what the Australian journalists made him out to be, and for one very simple reason.

Charles, Prince of Wales, was an inveterate *Goon Show* fan. Yes, that's right—a fan of *The Goon Show*. That's my argument for thinking he'd be a damn good king as well as a fine leader of the commonwealth of nations that had once been part of the British Empire. Why? Anyone who appreciates the hilarious logic and illogic of British comedian Spike Milligan's humor in that once-famous radio show had to be far more clever than stupid. Here's a quick story: Once when he was very old, Spike, who wrote the entire nine-year series of *The Goon Show*, received a telegram from the prince, honoring his contribution to British entertainment. The telegram was read out publicly, after which Spike grinned and growled, "The little groveling bastard!" The prince laughed this off, a sign of his generous good humor and heart. Spike was a refreshing tonic, a wild card, an iconoclast; his style of comedy was the grandfather of Monty Python. To love his humor was to enjoy a vision of life's absurdity, but with the relieving balm of laughter. Frankly, I prefer his absurdity to Samuel Beckett's; it's a lot more effective for being lighter—and as you know, often it's the real nincompoops who don't have much of a sense of humor. Of course, Beckett did—a dark one.

Charles has a good understanding of the complexity of the human condition; an understanding that brings a smile inside a grimace and one's teeth clenched inside a grin. It amuses me to hear the occasional journalist admit that when he or she actually meets Charles face-to-face at say, a royal reception, he turns out to be witty, charming, intelligent, and compassionate. In other words, he's not a clown, nor a goose, and definitely not a nincompoop.

How Prince Charles (and many another celebrities) gets reported on is an example to help explain what this book is about. Is it possible to know a person simply by reading about him? The example of Charles would suggest not. It's always going to be problematic getting to the truth of a person through written documents. It's difficult even when you're acquainted with the person!

Nonetheless, in this book I would like to find out about the historical character known as Jesus of Nazareth, in about the only way we can: simply by reading about him the way anyone who is unfamiliar with him might. Our focus for reflection will be the first book of the New Testament, the Gospel according to Matthew. If someone didn't know much about Jesus and wanted to find out more, this would logically be the first place to go: an original source, right at the front of the New Testament, which presents the life of Jesus.

Of course, the Gospel writers—the four men who wrote our primary-source accounts of Jesus' life on Earth—were favorable authorities. I don't deny it. This could have the result of skewing Jesus' portrait in an archly more positive light, the opposite of the "Prince Charles" problem. However, they claimed to be writing about God in a time when stating falsehoods about God would invite genuine mortal terror. So I would say that any "gilding of the lily" in these accounts of his life might be countered by the arrows of a profoundly accusatory conscience. People generally accept now, regardless of their various scepticisms about details, that there is a recognizable historical figure to be found at the center of the Gospels. There was a time when any tiny variation of detail from text to text of the four Gospels (written by Matthew, Mark, Luke, and John) prompted "Gotcha!"-like cries of triumph from conscientious non-believers and freethinkers. Now, in the cool light of a more relaxed secular culture, these details tend to be seen more as minor mysteries, rather than as ultimate deal breakers—at least by mainstream critics. Furthermore, we now tend to see history as a multifaceted reality, rather than a monolith: having four points of view on Jesus seems to fit our way of thinking about everything in the age of relativity, and life will always be a cubist painting rather than a Rubens. Additionally, Jesus was a teacher, and in the three years of his public ministry, he probably repeated himself as teachers do, with subtle variations depending upon his audience. No doubt, he found himself repeatedly in similar situations, and dealt with them in a variety of ways. Those variations have made their way into the accounts. If this is not the case, and the Gospels represent an early Christian propaganda campaign, then, based on the evidence, the organizers weren't very coordinated about it.

Nevertheless, this is the subject of theology and historiography. I'd better make it clear right away that the book before you now is not an exercise in theology nor historiography, at least, not consciously!

This book is more an exploration of simple affection and/or repulsion. I don't merely want to know about Jesus; I already know about him. Rather, I want to find out, by looking at one account of him, whether I like him. If this man were actually God and the account is a record of God's life on Earth, our emotional reaction to him, as opposed to our intellectual response, becomes tremendously important: Would we like God—simply like him, if we met him, heard him speak, and saw him in action?

Apropos, I have recently started to wonder which one is the better form of "faith": an intellectual assent to certain statements about Jesus, for example, "sacrifice" and "salvation," or a feeling of affection for Jesus—a simple liking of him? In the past, I have benefited from the intellectual clarification of ideas about Jesus and his mission, but growing older I have felt more a need to warm to him in order to want to keep doing as he says. After all, surely doing as he instructs is part of the necessary response of a person who calls himself a Christian; a disciple.

Oddly enough, boys and girls of the younger generation come at things through this simple realm of affection too. In the current Western world, with its complete absence of respect for authority and with its lack of guiding voices considered trustworthy, a younger generation has turned to simple first impressions as their guide. For them, merely "liking" something or someone is the starting point of all their responsiveness. It was not always this way.

I've always been attracted to Christianity. I was hopeless at sports at an all-boys Jesuit school, so I had to find something I was good at. Religion seemed a useful and less tiring option: the spirit was willing, but the flesh needed to sit down. Christianity sets the ethical bar comfortably low: the desire to do what is right trumps actually getting it right! Islam and Judaism both have a greater emphasis on law, obedience, and punishment. I've always preferred Christianity for its primary focus, which is mercy. I think this is a more realistic approach in the face of actual human behavior with its many faults.

Nevertheless, if I've been attracted to Christianity, would I actually be attracted to Jesus? Would his actual teachings and his personality—and his teachings are an expression of his personality—move me to affection for him, so much so that I would change the priorities of my life?

Would I like what he actually has to say?

Would I like him?

That's what we want to find out through this book, by going back to the start. Scholars will tell you that the placement of the books of the New Testament is not the same as the chronological order in which they were written, but the Gospel of Matthew is, as noted above, the first thing people find in the New Testament. (*The authorship of "Matthew"—that is, exactly who he was and even whether or not his actual name was Matthew—is not something I take up in this book. You can read all that for yourself if you're interested…and it is interesting, but….*) This book isn't a Bible commentary in any traditional sense. It's not a blow-by-blow analysis of the entire Gospel of Matthew. I retain the right to skip the boring bits.

It's just an attempt to find out if we would like Jesus from what he said and did. We take a few tools with us on the journey—some knowledge of history and of the other New Testament writings, but mostly we begin with curiosity, although I don't mind admitting that I would like to end in hope.

CHAPTER 1

AN ACT OF LOVE—NOT HIS

Her husband Joseph, being a righteous man and unwilling to expose her to public disgrace, planned to dismiss her quietly. (Matt 1:19)

Very few biographers can make the childhood of a celebrity interesting. Michael Caine managed it in his autobiography, so did Tom Baker (hilariously!) and Clive James. As readers, though, we want to get quickly to the things that made the adult person worth our attention. Furthermore, very few people have been famous for their childhoods alone.

The story of Jesus' childhood begins with an act of love—not his—his father's, that is, Joseph's. We know very little about Joseph, but, in Matthew's Gospel, we can tell in an instant that he would have made a tremendous dad. In the first chapter, Matthew tells us that Mary, Jesus' mother, was pledged to be married to Joseph, but then it was revealed that she was pregnant—and not by him. Joseph was immediately driven to call off the wedding. Who wouldn't be? But then Joseph slept on it. In a dream, we are told, an angel convinced him to go ahead with the marriage, and he did so. Apparently, the angel told Joseph that Mary had conceived by the Holy Spirit, and that the son to be born would "save his people from their sins."

Modern readers may scoff at the message. After all, it's a very precise "dream," isn't it? Think what you like about the specifics of the dream itself, but I do believe that Joseph could have woken up in the morning with a decision, having processed his concerns subconsciously during the night. The famous Broadway director, Harold Prince, who directed *The Phantom of the Opera* amongst other superhits, once said that when he had a problem directing a scene, he would read the script just before going to bed, concentrate on the problem, flick off the light, and usually as a result of a good night's subconsciousness, he would wake with a solution. Many people recount similar subliminal processes in sleep.

Joseph's action after the dream is a heroic act of love. In a small village, Joseph faced derision and social exclusion alongside his prematurely pregnant betrothed. However, he went through with the marriage. He ignored the crowd for the sake of love.

It moves me when I see those stalwart friends of an accused person in a court case, you know, the ones who march down the street side by side with the offender, prepared to be seen on national television supporting the criminal outcast. It would be so easy to stay at home, go with him in "spirit," and disassociate oneself from the pariah. These friends understand the complexity of life and know that a single crime or a single verdict is not the final word on a person's true character. With great strength of character, they nail their colors to the mast, even when the mast is sinking.

This is admirable, yes? Well, that's the kind of public disgrace Joseph was prepared to endure out of love for Mary.

Nor was Jesus' infancy without extraordinary demands on Joseph and Mary. King Herod of Judea, the local despot, got wind that a pretender to his throne had been born somewhere in his territory. Rumors, which concerned the birth of baby Jesus, were swirling around. Some astronomers from Persia came looking for a newborn "king,"—you know, the "star of Bethlehem" story, the "three wise men," and all that—and Herod was alerted to a possible threat. He decided to wipe out all newborn males under the age of two.

It's surprising that some people doubt this story of mass slaughter because, they say, there is no independent corroboration of the story in other historical documents. They treat it as if it were some melodramatic elaboration, a juicy piece of fabrication to make the story more heroic. I grew up in Australia in the 1960s and '70s. A more placid period and place in history would be hard to find, and for many people as I grew up, such an outrage as Herod's would be emblazoned across the historical records of the world!

Rubbish. It's just the sort of bargain basement behavior tyrants indulge in with horrific regularity throughout history, and nobody breathes a word.

It's amazing how often when studying a Gospel one hears that this or that episode must have been invented by Jesus' followers, because it couldn't have really happened. Indeed, some people think that most of the Gospel written by John is pure fabrication. The strange thing is that it's always the most interesting events people say are made up! It's as if the book had one of the greatest editors in history, a novelist of the most imaginative powers standing by to "goose up" proceedings when things get dull. In the theatre, such a person might be called a dramaturge or play doctor. I would love to have met this extraordinary person—or persons, if it were a committee! The theory has two slight flaws. First, it begs the question: Why would these inventive types lavish such imagination upon a story that must have been so boring without them? And second, their inventiveness makes them so close to a god themselves that we may as well worship *them*!

In the context of the approaching threat of Herod, Joseph had another dream, and woke with a solution: he bundled his family off to Egypt and out of the king's clutches just in time (see Matt 2). People have often made the point that, in his infancy, Jesus became a refugee, and for many Christians this evokes empathy for modern refugees, for we live in a time of great upheaval of populations around the world, and so many stateless people are in need of compassion. Jesus would have suffered as a child refugee suffers. This is important to remember, because if we believe that he was God, then even the tiniest suffering was a terrible lesson to him about the physical and psychological realities of the human condition.

However, his experience of the situation as a child would have been nothing compared to the anguish of his refugee parents, wondering what would become of their dear son. Parents must suffer as adults, fully aware of their powerlessness in a way that a child is not. Joseph and Mary suffered that anguish. Theirs was an extremely painful experience of early parenthood.

Eventually, once again with the aid of dreams, and upon hearing of Herod's widely unlamented death, Joseph decided to return his family to Israel, but settled in Nazareth, a town in Galilee, which was far north of Judea, where Herod's son was now reigning, and so, Joseph believed, well out of harm's way.

These later actions of Joseph show him to be a strong man, but they are actions of necessity. What made Joseph a great dad was his initial choice to remain loyal to Mary in her time of need; an act of the deepest and most selfless love.

I like that. I like Jesus' dad.

I also like a book when chapter one is brief—like this one!—and especially when it's about a person's childhood.

CHAPTER 2

NEW MAN ON THE BLOCK

Isn't it awful when you sit down in a public place and realize you have inadvertently chosen the seat close to the smelly person? The beautiful St. Patrick's Church in Sydney is across from an inner-city park and many a homeless gent or lady likes to seek shelter inside the church when the weather turns sour. Slowly the aroma of last week's urine starts to waft across to the pew where I am sitting, and every charitable instinct ekes out of my bones the more the delightful odor takes hold! In Canberra, I once got on a bus destined for Sydney only to discover that I was sitting next to what seemed to be a denizen of all the five-star garbage bins of the nation's capital. What's more, he was the friendly type, and the instant I sat down, he turned, presented his hand to me and grinned, "Well, I'm Fred," as if it were going to be the beginning of a beautiful friendship. Camera shot: bird's eye view, zooming out to the universe as I throw back my head and scream at the top of my lungs in the spirit of Edvard Munch!

I think my reaction to John the Baptist would have been the same. I can admire him from a distance—a very great distance, but I can't like him. It's my prejudice. I have a natural aversion to dirty, smelly zealots. John did weird things: he wore clothes made of camel's hair, and he lived on a diet of locusts and wild honey. The wild honey I could take. The locusts? Get me outta here! That's not to say that such people don't do tremendous good, don't shake the world, wake it up, and make it better. They do. It's just that they make me deeply uncomfortable, and it's hard to like someone who makes you want to vomit.

5

WOULD I *LIKE* JESUS?

John's message was one with which we've all now become famil-iar, if only from movies where religious zealots walk down the street wearing sandwich boards with doom-laden predictions on them: "Repent, for the kingdom of heaven is near!" John's methods of draw-ing attention to himself were unorthodox: he started preaching in the desert, and people had to come all the way to him. In other words, they must have already wanted a big change in their lives even to go and listen to his ideas. This means that he wasn't for the mainstream; he was for the fringe dwellers in society, the already seriously dis-gruntled. (The word *disgruntled* has always struck me as odd. Do we ever meet a person who is "gruntled"?) According to Matthew, John preceded Jesus as a preacher and even baptized him (see Matt 3) in rather exceptional circumstances. (*I wonder if all that standing in the River Jordan made John the Baptist stink any less. Perhaps, from the waist down….*)

It would have been quite a day on the banks of the River Jordan: this nobody comes along, John baptizes him, and the next thing you know, the sky is cracked open and a glowing dove flies down and a voice booms out that this nobody, Jesus, is the one that you've all been waiting for, the Messiah, the Son of David, the Son of God. Yep. That would have been a real barbecue stopper around old Jerusalem–town! After Jesus' baptism, John shrinks in importance and the crowds start paying attention to the newcomer. Had John been a modern advertising executive, he would have realized he'd made the biggest mistake in his life: introducing the new model Messiah—from a differ-ent company!

However, Jesus doesn't quite yet command the spotlight. First, he retreats to the desert and faces three significant temptations. This is the moment at which Jesus begins to reveal his own character. This is when he is no longer a protected child or just someone in the crowd waiting for baptism, but he becomes instead a dynamo (see Matt 4).

The story is written in symbolic language. If it had been a Wagnerian opera, it would have been written in three almighty, long acts. Wagner didn't require many characters to write epic confronta-tions; he knew that the true story always resides in the invisible seis-mology of a character's soul, and the strata involved go all the way down to hell and all the way up to heaven. For him, every tale was necessarily going to be a long journey and take a long time to be completed. Like a Wagner opera, the temptations of Jesus have language on the top like the lip of a volcano, and a subtext as deep as the earth's core.

At first the "tempter" comes to Jesus when he is hungry and suggests that, since he is God, why doesn't he just turn some stones into bread? However, the hunger was no accident. Jesus was deliberately starving himself to become stronger. "What does not destroy me makes me stronger," as Nietzsche famously said in latter days. (*Nietzsche himself went mad and wound up in an asylum, so whatever it was he was up against, it didn't destroy him but it certainly didn't make him stronger.*)

Have you ever been really, really hungry—starvation-like hungry? I haven't. "The only way to get rid of temptation is to yield to it," to quote Oscar Wilde. For me, to be hungry means to eat—immediately! Furthermore, in the overabundance of the modern Western world, to eat is no more difficult than a quick race to the nearest McDonald's, if one is really desperate! In the West, we run from discomfort and from physical stress, except when it leads to material glory, such as in athletic training and in Olympic games. But Jesus has been fasting for days, with deliberate concentration on denying himself one of the simple delights of this world—daily meals. So the devil tempts Jesus with the simplest of comforts: physical comfort, the relief of pain, the satisfaction of ordinary food. Centuries later Gerard Manley Hopkins, the celebrated Jesuit poet and depressive, would describe such relief as "Carrion Comfort," meaning despair. We tend to think of despair as being like depression. While the two may be cousins, they are not the same. Depression is almost always painful. Despair, in fact, can be very comfortable. Despair is the surrender of spiritual priorities for the sake of material ease (more on this later!), and this is the very thing Jesus is training himself not to do.

Jesus rejects the temptation firmly. "One does not live by bread alone," he quotes from traditional Jewish writings, "but by every word that comes from the mouth of God" (Matt 4:4). He isn't prepared to settle for short-term material reward when something far better for the spirit is a little further off. Why settle for McDonald's when there's a spiritual gourmet chef waiting a little further up the road?

OK, so that doesn't work. Next, the devil takes him to the top of the temple in Jerusalem, and questions his bona fides. "If you are the Son of God, throw yourself down" (Matt 4:6). The assumption is that Jesus would be saved from harm by angels, who would come and set him down gently. It seems such a little thing. Why not do it and make the devil shut up and go away? What is the temptation?

It is hijinks—a sort of self-satisfying merrymaking with no point.

In *Doctor Faustus*, the sixteenth-century play by Christopher Marlowe, a philosopher named Faustus is granted magical powers by the devil, and spends most of the play simply pulling practical jokes and doing pranks, that is, when he isn't lamenting his profound and terminal fall from grace. It's an uneven play, partly because the sense of spiritual barrenness is so great and comes so early, that Marlowe seems desperate to find comical ways to keep the audience interested for the rest of the duration, but also partly because the gift of the devil has permanently imbalanced Faustus as a personality: if you're so powerful, you can do whatever you like, even stupid things. That's what becomes of Faustus; he becomes endlessly mischievous and his life becomes pointless. In Matthew, the devil is offering Jesus the chance to become a kind of infantile Superman, racing the train for the heck of it, or batting the ball all the way to Venus, or leaping tall buildings in a single bound. However, the price is too great, like the price Faustus pays; it is a loss of integrity, of an integrated personality. If Jesus had accepted the offer, his entire ministry would have carried the taint of triviality, and would have seemed contingent upon whim. Jesus' work would have borne the patina of showmanship, and he would have toppled into the role of yet one more meretricious glory seeker.

Jesus resists the devil with sobriety: "Do not put the Lord your God to the test" (Matt 4:7).

So the devil next takes him, we are told, to the top of a tall mountain and shows him all the kingdoms of the world, and says that he will give Jesus all these powerful places, if only Jesus will worship him. It's quite an offer: absolute power on earth. How many leaders—Caesar, Napoleon, and Hitler—have wanted this? Forget them! How many people who you know have wanted this in their secret and unknown hearts? In theory, Jesus wouldn't be such a bad ruler. It would have been easy for Jesus to rationalize, "Well, I could do a lot of good, and

I could replace a lot of cruel despots out there in those kingdoms." It's a damn good offer. The devil doesn't gamble with tokens; he always makes temptation sound like a good idea!

The problem is the *condition*. To achieve this mastery of the bodies politic, Jesus must first worship the devil, and Jesus knows that worship is the reserved right of God. Jesus was being asked to settle for something lesser; the power being offered is a limited one, and the condition is a demeaning one. Like in the temptation of the bread, Jesus is being asked to make a fundamental choice between the benefits of material things—the kingdoms of *this* world—or spiritual things—the kingdom of heaven.

Jesus responds, "Away with you, Satan! for it is written, 'Worship the Lord your God, and serve only him'" (Matt 4:10).

He makes the choice for heaven, a damned hard one. How many politicians have chosen the alternative in their heart of hearts?

This episode of the temptations is unlike anything else in Matthew's account. It feels like the inspiration for a thousand sequences in Hollywood films that have nothing to do with Jesus. It's surreal, and heroic; a titanic first encounter between protagonist and antagonist, prefiguring in symbolic terms the struggle to be played out subsequently in realistic ones. It cries out for enormous, color-drenched paintings to be made of it; it demands triptychs that would cover the walls of cathedrals. It is Sherlock Holmes and Professor Moriarty at the Reichenbach Falls. It is Pompey and Caesar, Churchill and Hitler, Valjean and Javert. It is bold, and essential, and dare I say, romantic. It is timeless in its depopulated landscape and its sense of taking place on a higher plane: these two alone seem to be forging the destiny of the world in an invisible clash of spirits. The Jesus who emerges is bold, resolute, committed, and has a sense of mission that cannot be shaken.

The Jesus who is portrayed here is the same one who will later defy the high priests of Jerusalem and the Roman governor, Pontius Pilate, in scenes that are rooted in historicity and presented realistically. There as here, he comes across as knowing his own mind with an inner strength that will see him make choices that are right, as opposed to choices that are expedient.

It is in these symbolic scenes, in this apparent psychodrama at the start of his public career, that Jesus already starts looking like a man able to claim a towering place in world history, not as a hedonist, not as an inconsequential clown, and not as an *imperator*, a political leader of nations. He is starkly presented as a man who will do right because it is right.

This will make him instantly and immensely dangerous to the conventionally powerful who buy glory through fear or favor. He will stand up against any tide of popular opinion.

This makes him resemble his dad, and you've got to like that.

CHAPTER 3

THE BIG ONE

Well, not quite the big one yet. What's the big one? The Sermon on the Mount, that's the big one.

Before that, Jesus takes four significant actions: He moves away from home; he begins to preach a new philosophy or "message" (a "message" generally demands a more active response than does a "philosophy"); he gathers a group of assistants; and he begins healing the sick.

His move is to a town called Capernaum. It's on the Sea of Galilee. It's close to the town of Magdala, where Mary Magdalene (ever heard of her?) is from. Why did Jesus choose to go there? I don't know. I suspect the ground there was fertile for new ideas. It had a fishing industry. My dad used to say that every fisherman must be a philosopher; all that waiting around in a mist of uncertainty, and at dawn too, when each day bears promise or dread; it turns one into a thinker. In this context, Jesus' message must have resonated: "Repent, for the kingdom of heaven has come near." What's interesting is that this was John the Baptist's catch-cry too. However, Jesus isn't going out into the desert to preach it; he's going to the towns. He's going into society, not away from it. He's trying a different approach, and it makes all the difference in the world. He doesn't wait for the people to come to him on the fringe. Instead, he catches them in their homes; in their workplaces. It makes matters of faith completely and utterly mundane, in the sense of being integrated into the ordinary daily life of ordinary, mainstream people.

That's where he meets his first assistants, in their workplace. He finds Peter and Andrew in the midst of their fishing trade. There's a wonderful passage:

> As he walked by the Sea of Galilee, he saw two brothers, Simon, who is called Peter, and Andrew his brother, casting a net into the sea—for they were fishermen. And he said to them, "Follow me, and I will make you fish for people." Immediately they left their nets and followed him. (Matt 4:18–20)

The passage, as a piece of writing, has wonderful examples of antithesis. There is Jesus walking, a free spirit taking in the shoreline, and there are the brothers laboring against nature. They are intent on business; he enters their lives as the visionary. They pursue fish; he turns their attention to souls. The passage has the brevity of poetry. Many a historian will later analyze it for socioeconomic veracity and for cultural insight and so on. Many a preacher will extrapolate some finer points of theology from it. None of those extra words will come near to equaling the satisfying directness of the original. In some way, extra words will confuse the issue, for what we have here, simply, is Jesus' power. He takes ordinary citizens, not radicals, and he rearranges their priorities. Later, Peter will continue to show all the doubts and fears that a sensible person would have about the project. Peter isn't crazy. Later, when things aren't going well, he complains that "we left everything to follow you!" and we know how he feels: there he was, minding his own business, when Jesus blew in and swept them up in his dream.

This persuasive power of Jesus precedes his power of physical healing. Matthew tells us that he begins to preach, and only then he begins to cure. He goes about the region of Galilee preaching "the good news of the kingdom," and, as a result of his message, people come to him who have diseases or suffer from seizures and paralysis, and he heals them.

> Jesus went throughout Galilee, teaching in their synagogues and proclaiming the good news of the kingdom and curing every disease and every sickness among the people. (Matt 4:23)

12

However, it seems as if word of the cures begins to spread faster than word of the kingdom: soon people are rolling in from as far away as Jerusalem. In fact, the crowds become a problem. People, even the best of them, are fickle. Think how readily we show enthusiasm for an influential person who has a solution to our problems, right there and then on the spot; at that moment, we'll say and do anything to get what we want from him or her, not thinking for a moment about what that person or his or her philosophy may mean to us otherwise. Once our problems are solved, we forget them, faster than the speed of thought! Years later, we may even have forgotten the incident itself that brought us into their sphere. So often, once we have what we need, our lives—our priorities and values—really don't change all that much.

Realizing that a lot of the crowd is not there to adopt his ideas, Jesus retreats up a mountain, sits his assistants down with him, and clarifies his teachings for them. It's a sensible move. The crowds have swollen to the extent that he now needs to engage other voices as well as his own to preach the message. In fact, as Matthew later says, the crowds catch up with him on the mountain, gather around, and listen in as well. He must first train his assistants, his "disciples," or else the crowds will exhaust him, and they will merely go away healed, but essentially unchanged at heart.

This training program, which we now call "The Sermon on the Mount," is, without doubt, the most lunatic speech ever spoken by a sane man. Monty Python sent it up by having people at the rear of the crowd misunderstand "Blessed are the cheese makers" for "Blessed are the peacemakers," but the ideas Jesus presents are mad enough that they don't require Monty Python's help to render them absurd. However, although the ideas are mad, the deliverer himself is not mad; this is the paradox of the Sermon on the Mount. The language used smacks of sobriety, intelligence, and insight into human nature. Nor does Jesus come across as a zealot. The program is not an ideology, in the same way that Nazism or communism or even capitalism is a fixed set of dictums to be enforced. It speaks to individual hearts about actions a person may do, rather than to whole nations about how programs and policies may be rethought so as to restructure society. It is about everyday situations, rather than radical worldwide transformation—even if by extrapolation it could lead to that. It is almost like those ads that say, "You can try this at home." It is a program aimed at the individual rather than at society as a whole. What's crazy about it is that the sermon contradicts everything we ever thought about how to live a satisfactory life on this earth.

For example, I was at a country wedding a few years ago. Behind me were a young father and his two boys. We were sitting in a Christian church. While we were waiting for the ceremony to get underway, one boy hit the other. The father advised the victim, "You hit him back now, and then you'll both be square. You'll feel good, and he won't hit you again." I couldn't believe that anybody, let alone a father, could so unashamedly give this advice, especially while sitting in a church. However, I realized that, in essence, this was the advice that rules the world. It represents how most people think and behave most of the time. Revenge, seen as fairness, is the oldest idea in the book. The fact that it doesn't work is the subject of half the world's literature, and the cause of virtually all the world's problems, but that still doesn't stop it from being the most common advice given. You could say that *that* idea is mad, but it's conventional, and that father sitting in that church, giving normal and demonstrably mad advice, had clearly no clue about Christianity whatsoever. The Sermon on the Mount utterly contradicts what that father believed is sensible human behavior.

> Blessed are the poor in spirit, for theirs is the kingdom
> of heaven.
> Blessed are those who mourn, for they will be comforted.
> Blessed are the meek, for they will inherit the earth.
> Blessed are those who hunger and thirst for righteousness,
> for they will be filled.
> Blessed are the merciful, for they will receive mercy.
> Blessed are the pure in heart, for they will see God.
> Blessed are the peacemakers, for they will be called children
> of God.
> Blessed are those who are persecuted for righteousness' sake,
> For theirs is the kingdom of heaven.
>
> (Matt 5:3–10)

Jesus begins with a litany of encouragement, a series of statements we know as the Beatitudes. Are you feeling down or "poor in spirit"? The kingdom of heaven belongs to you! Are you perhaps suffering a loss and grieving? You will be comforted! Are you the sort of person who stands back and lets the bully push past? The whole earth will be given to you! Do you want to see justice done and righteousness triumph? You'll see it! Do you forgive people, and are you a "merciful" person? If so, then when you do something wrong, God is going to be merciful to you! Do you do good things from clear, pure motives? You will see God! Are you someone who works for peace? You are virtually sons and daughters of God! Are you being persecuted because you do what is right? You're going to share the kingdom of heaven with the people who are poor in spirit!

By making these statements, it seems as if Jesus was not just encouraging people who currently did these things, but also painting a portrait of the behaviors he wanted to see in people who would be his followers. I don't mean the mourning and the feeling down, but being meek and being merciful, thirsting for righteousness and working for peace and so on. What's interesting is that these behaviors are not highly valued in the world. They are given lip service, but they are not things that are generally rewarded, and they are seldom the modus operandi of people whom society tends to laud as successes. ("It's not the *earth* the meek inherit, it's the *dirt!*" to quote Mordred in the musical *Camelot.*) The human tradition is one that honors ambition, drive, toughness, and cleverness. Getting away with things is secretly smiled upon. Parents will tend to admire a child more if he or she pushes through to the front, and they will downplay any nefarious activity that may have helped bring about that result. Call it human nature. The famed British scientist Richard Dawkins would say that it's just the selfish gene going about its routine selfishness. Behind Jesus' recommendations is an essential demand of faith: he isn't promising short-term material rewards, but rather, long-term spiritual ones, so you're going to have to believe in rewards you can't actually see, while you're still living in this world. That's faith.

Are there to be no benefits now? These statements come at the beginning of the sermon. By the end, Jesus is encouraging people to act on his words and not just sit there and admire them, and saying that the rewards of active implementation are immediate:

> "Everyone then who hears these words of mine and acts on them will be like a wise man who built his house on rock….And everyone who hears these words of mine and does not act on them will be like a foolish man who built his house on sand." (Matt 7:24, 26)

The image he uses is of a fierce storm, battering both houses and, of course, washing away the house built on indolence. It seems as if acting on Jesus' words will actually bring about positive consequences for the believer, a sense of living in the kingdom of God, now. It could be argued that this is selfish and that Christianity is supposed to be about denying the self for the sake of others. Well, if it is selfishness, it's not the conventional selfishness that seeks material rewards; it's not the way that the world works itself into its usual misguided misery!

I've never been one for mere philosophy. I know it has its place, a crucial place worthy of the expansiveness of the human mind; and reflection about life is one of the human gifts. However, I prefer active teaching, or rather, teaching for action, at least when it comes to matters of ethics. Jesus doesn't teach a static philosophy: "Not everyone who says to me 'Lord, Lord,' will enter the kingdom of heaven, but only the one who *does* the will of my Father." (Matt 7:21). He seems to believe that the way to a better world is not through sitting and asking, "What is better?" but rather through getting up and treating each other better. So, if Jesus were a philosopher, he's a philosopher who preaches action.

For what it's worth, I like that.

CHAPTER 4

MORE OF THE BIG ONE

You didn't really think we could skip over the rest of the sermon just like that, did you? It's too interesting and too crazy.

Yes, it's crazy…and we've got two thousand years of extra history to prove it, by and large, because humanity has not implemented this way of behaving. Individuals in governments have, certain people in authority have, some in the churches have, and numbers of ordinary individuals in society have. However, if one considers the terrible *inhumanity* of humanity, of which the history books are replete, it seems as if human nature has rejected as useless Jesus' ideas on how to behave. No doubt this is why the world is now a utopian paradise of war, murder, corruption, betrayal, and despair!

Jesus goes on to specify further behaviors he wants to see in his followers, but first he must do two more things to lay the groundwork.

"You are the salt of the earth….You are the light of the world." (Matt 5:13, 14)

We have seen that Jesus began his speech by encouraging his followers, who are ordinary people, many of whom would have suffered low self-esteem: farmers and fishermen—people who have seen the highs and lows, but mostly lows. The next thing grows out of that first step: now, he tells them that they have a light worth shining in the world, and that they are the "salt of the earth." Nowadays, when this phrase is used to describe someone, it usually means that the person being referred to is decent and hard-working; somebody reliable and reasonably well-intentioned. This isn't what Jesus is saying. In his time, salt was a *preservative*; something that kept things fresh and uncorrupted, a good thing, a life-giving agent. Jesus is saying that his disciples have within them the power to refresh the lives of the people around them. Thus, from encouragement he has moved to praise. Good move! Have you ever known an audience that didn't respond well to a little bit of buttering up? They'll be happy to listen further.

"Do not think that I have come to abolish the law or the prophets; I have come not to abolish but to fulfill." (Matt 5:17)

The next move is a clever one on Jesus' part. Such preachers faced opposition from groups of self-appointed religious experts who saw their job as supervising Old Testament law and who would naturally want to check if this new man on the block was touting a drift away from it. They were elitists, who liked to make out that their strict adherence to the law made them superior. Naturally, amongst the ordinary people of the day—those very crowds who kept coming to him—would also be conservatives who depended upon the status quo for their sense of security; these would be ready to turn their backs on him if they thought he was ripping up the constitution, so to speak. Furthermore, there would have been extremists in the crowd; they would not need much urging to smash the social barriers and tear up the social floorboards. The area Jesus was in, the region of Galilee, had already produced notorious rebels. For instance, Judas of Galilee was a Jewish leader who had led an armed resistance to the census imposed for Roman tax purposes by the provincial governor Quirinius at about the time of Jesus' birth. The revolt was crushed and Judas was killed, but the anti-Roman revolutionary spirit did not die. The extremists were like oil just waiting to be ignited.

Not much has changed. Preachers are still dealing with a mixture of religious elitists, conservatives, and hotheads in their congregations.

Elitists. I remember a few years ago a priest saying over lunch that he knew individuals in his parish were reporting the content of his sermons to the bishop in the hope of getting him into trouble. He was an old priest, but that didn't make him narrow in his views, and these spies were from a group who regarded themselves as the true core of the Catholic Church. The priest shrugged off the threat and continued in his role until he retired at the natural time. His bishop took no action against him, demonstrating either good sense by ignoring the troublemakers, or else a miraculous ineffectualness! (If so, one hopes it stemmed from the Beatitude of meekness!)

Conservatives. There are a lot of people drawn to religion out of a love of ritual and its reassuring lack of change. Sometimes the initial impulse of faith that brings them to the ritual gets lost through sheer habit, and it is replaced with a fear of change itself. Thus, they resent anyone who reminds them of the impulsiveness of faith, because any impulse will always challenge the kind of religious fossilization into which they have fallen. Here, I don't point the finger at a particular group, for we are all liable to cherish the comfort of the familiar, the reassurance of sameness, and ritual by its nature has that attraction in it.

During the 1960s (the swinging '60s!) the Catholic Church underwent a dramatic (dare I say radical?) change as a result of a meeting of its leadership known as the Second Vatican Council. There were quite a few amongst the leadership who resented the change, which was pushed through by two pioneering popes, John XXIII and Paul VI. After this gathering at the Vatican, ordinary people—"laity"—were handing out communion the way only priests used to be allowed to; the traditional language of the Church—Latin—was replaced with local "vernacular" languages, which people could understand. Even the altar rail, which separated the congregation from the sanctuary around the altar, was removed!

It must have been very hard for many of the older generation to accept such changes, which would have felt like the floorboards were being ripped up beneath their feet. To this day, some in the Catholic Church have continued to feel that the changes went too far and that something of the majesty of church ritual—its specialness in their lives—was irrevocably lost. Most recently, the Catholic Mass has seen some traditional language—translated from the Latin—restored to its text. While it's good to have the same prayers reflected across the whole world, so that travelers can join in the ritual of the Mass anywhere they go, faith, it seems to me, resists gentrification, even in language, and wherever possible it's good for faith to be rendered in contemporary terms. Sometimes we need to be reminded that Jesus never even used the words *thee* or *thou* or their archaic equivalent in Aramaic. A large part of his appeal, as I've said elsewhere, was in his use of the colloquial.

I don't want to give the impression that it is only the Catholic Church that has conservatives in it. Presbyterian Church communities have been known to debate whether guitar music should be allowed to replace the organ! And look at the struggles that the worldwide Anglican communion are having over acceptance or rejection of gay marriage. Conservatives are not automatically a bad thing. They can be a blessing and a curse: a blessing, because the older ones—and not all conservatives are old—carry the corporate history and the younger ones have the energy to remind us of lasting principles before they get lost; and a curse, when they enforce mere habit at the expense of inspiration.

Hotheads. There will always be hotheads in religion. There will always be some who are absolutely on fire for violent change, and need cooling. In this era of international religious terrorism, this fact is known too well; but history tells us that it has always been the case. In the time of Jesus, there was a group called "zealots." Arguably, they were a bunch of early religious extremists. They would have been listening to see if Jesus was a staunch defender of Judaism, and the Jewish religious culture.

Such types—elitists, conservatives, and hotheads—would have been sitting within the crowds to whom Jesus and his followers were preaching.

Now, Jesus was prepared to go beyond the traditional Jewish law, which had bound the society together for centuries, and institute a bold new way of thinking about God and about people's relationship to him, based not on law but on love. In this sermon and his subsequent preaching, he will go on to claim that "sin" is a fundamental condition of humanity and not simply a matter of legal breaches; he will shift the basis of human thinking about right and wrong from questions of actions and outcomes to the question of *intention*, and he will cut through to the heart of human nature.

He makes clear to his listeners, who by now are made up of his disciples and the crowds who have come up the mountainside to join them, that he is definitely not going to tear up the law. He is not about to smash the basis of all Jewish society. Conservatives and radicals can cool it: he is not going to uproot the basic way of life of society.

However, his followers are going to have to meet a test of righteousness that "surpasses" even that of the legal experts (known in his culture as the "Pharisees") and the people who taught the law. That test would be something that goes far beyond merely following rules.

He's walking a tightrope without a safety net! He has to outline his bold new approach.

> "You have heard that it was said to those of ancient times, 'You shall not murder'; and 'whoever murders shall be liable to judgment.' But I say to you that if you are angry with a brother or sister, you will be liable to judgment." (Matt 5:21–22)

When he outlines the new approach, wow! It comes in a series of ethical punches like no other before it; the list is a veritable Manny Pacquiao of knock-out hits to the conventional moral chin. What is Jesus' attitude to murder? You shouldn't even be angry with your "brother"; that's already a sin. (He means selfish anger, the kind of anger that leads to murder.) Adultery? You've already committed it, he says to the men, just by looking lustfully at another woman. Divorce? It's not just a matter of some legal papers and saying goodbye to the wife: the man who divorces his wife hurts her deeply, forcing her to become an adulteress. (He's very realistic about people's sexual needs.) What about the old adage: "An eye for an eye, a tooth for a tooth"? It has no place in Christianity. Instead, when confronted by the bully or the oppressor, give them everything they ask for and more; shower them with your acquiescence. However, this does not mean that one ignores injustices to others, as he makes clear later. Enemies? We must love them, pray for them, and do good to them. Why? Because God, the Father, gives good things even to evil people, and you, he says to his followers, must "be perfect, therefore, as your heavenly Father is perfect" (Matt 5:48).

It is in this last section that I admire his thinking most of all: "For if you love those who love you, what reward do you have?" (Matt 5:46). *Love* here means not just a feeling; it means first, doing good to a wide range of people: It can be something you do to friends, family, and supporters—your "network." However, it should extend even beyond this. "Enemies" are natural foes; people whose interests compete with yours and those of your network. They could be members of another political party or another faction within a political party; they could be other tribes, or other families; people in one social class may see themselves as the enemy of the people in another. Jesus is putting forward a fundamentally new principle of fairness and justice. He bases it on the idea that God provides sunshine and rain to both good and bad people (in an agrarian society, the necessary elements that nurtured good crops were seen as a free gift from God, and were available to all). Thus, being "perfect" meant seeing your enemies not as rivals but, more objectively, as people who held equal rights as yourself in the sight of God. We are starting to see another fundamental characteristic to be adopted by a follower of Jesus. He has called on his disciples to be merciful, to thirst for justice, to be peacemakers. Now he calls on them to "do" love—*do* it, not necessarily *feel* it—even to enemies.

In summary, he seems to be warning against a complacent love, where you only do good amongst your own group because they're the ones who are most likely to give you something in return—a kind of "quid-pro-quo" form of love. There is also another danger he wants to address: boasting about the good that you do, and showing off about it. In modern times, for example, corporations do this sort of thing all the time; it's called sponsorship, which is another form of advertising. When we boast about the good things we do, all we're really doing is expanding the reach of the quid-pro-quo love against which Jesus was warning his audience. That isn't what Jesus means by "love" or "doing good"; his entire emphasis is on serving other people for their sake, not ours. We must be genuinely concerned for the well-being of our enemies' souls. It is reminiscent of a wonderful prayer Catholics say at the end of the Rosary: "O my Jesus…lead all souls to heaven *especially those in most need of your Mercy*." So, sounding a cautionary note, he says, don't do good things for the sake of public adulation.

> "Beware of practicing your piety before others in order to be seen by them; for then you have no reward from your Father in heaven." (Matt 6:1)

Pretentious piety is anathema. He's seen enough of that kind of narcissism. You want to do good? Then do it as secretly as possible. Do it in such a way that God sees it; no one else's approbation matters. I am reminded of Sir Thomas More's advice to young Rich in Robert Bolt's play *A Man for All Seasons*. Rich wants to be promoted to court. More tells him that he should remain a school teacher, his current profession. Rich asks who will ever know he has done any good in a classroom. "God and your students will; that's a pretty good audience," More replies. According to Jesus, the temptation to conspicuous charity is devilish. Oh, you may shine your light, or rather, "let" your light shine before others—a less deliberate act (see Matt 5)—but your purpose is not to draw glory to yourself (see Matt 6). Furthermore, he has a wonderful metaphor: When you give to the needy, "do not let your left hand know what your right hand is doing," in other words, don't dwell upon your goodness and puff yourself up about it; move on, selflessly and self-effacingly.

Some people might say that Jesus was mad, meaning too idealistic; Don Quixote-like mad. In fact, I started this chapter saying this sermon is crazy. I was being provocative. It's only crazy in so far as "normal" human behavior does not follow the pattern prescribed in it. However, just imagine what a world we would have, if this *were* the pattern of human behavior. How different would this benighted planet be? A place where people showed kindness to their enemies, and didn't expect adulation and reward in return? A place where people were merciful to each other, and made peace their priority? Why haven't we done this? Think of the daily aggravations that would disappear—no road rage! Think of how crime would be reduced. What would happen if enemy gangs took up the guidance of Jesus? Wouldn't they themselves be relieved? Think of how world conflicts would be healed. It is an ideal, and yet it's not so pie-in-the-sky. In the 1980s a group of radical Catholic and Protestant citizens in Northern Ireland began holding prayer services together, and forgave each other for the bombings, knifings, and shootings that members of their denominations had done. American President Jimmy Carter took the initiative to broker a peace between Egypt and Israel in 1978, and even quoted the words, "Blessed are the peacemakers…" when the deal was signed. Jesus' advice seems to work when it's tried. It's not often tried.

Human nature is very strong. The survival instinct as well as the instinct of pride and greed for supremacy stand in the way of implementing Jesus' program. In order to put it into practice, there needs to be a more fundamental change of priorities: there must be a belief that long-term spiritual gain is worth short-term material surrender. It becomes clearer how strong Jesus was in resisting the temptations of the devil, for this was the same choice that he faced. It's the choice we all face. We have to give up the things most people cling to the hardest. However, we can imagine the result—so why don't we? It's an amazing program for personal transformation, isn't it? Divine, I fear, but also, in a way, isn't it just common sense?

The Sermon on the Mount is not over. Can you stand some more?

The next topic is prayer. It follows from what Jesus has just said. Don't show off about your charity, and don't show off about your prayer. How about those Sunday television preachers who bellow and scream their prayers and boast about millions watching their TV shows around the world? Jesus is not interested in grandiose words or outsized gestures for all to see; you don't need to speak like a bargain basement Shakespeare with the "thees," "thines," and "thys" to get God's attention. Use simple words, and in private too. He gives his listeners an example of how to pray:

> Our Father in heaven,
>   hallowed be your name.
>   Your kingdom come.
>   Your will be done,
>   on earth as it is in heaven.
>   Give us this day our daily bread.
>   And *forgive us our debts*
>   *as we also have forgiven our debtors*
> (Matt 6:9–12, emphasis added)

That last line is the killer! There is a condition to his mercy. God's love may be unconditional—any parent's love is! If you bring 'em into the world, you can't stop loving 'em; it's one of the "natural" things about God; but his mercy depends upon our being merciful to others. And with good reason, it seems to me. If someone is not merciful, he or she doesn't know the value of mercy, and isn't likely to go asking for it from God. Elsewhere, Jesus tells us that a woman of easy virtue who wept and washed his feet with her tears was forgiven her sins because she loved much. The passage might also mean: you can tell she's *been* forgiven, because she shows so much love to someone else. Love and mercy—*compassionate care*, to use another phrase or *charity* to use a more familiar one—come from a tender heart; and "tender" always implies something wounded but made richer because of it. The merciful always understand the need for mercy from their experience.

There is a temptation to lock in the words of the Lord's Prayer, this simple prayer quoted above, so that it can become something of a formula, rather than an example. However, it is only an example. A fine one, certainly, because it focuses on what Jesus believes is important to our lives: God's will, our daily needs, and forgiveness. All our prayers can benefit from including these essentials, but our prayers do not need to be formal, rigid, or ritualized. Here, Jesus frees us to feel confident in praying our own words from the heart. Jesus democratized prayer and by so doing, virtually democratized God.

Getting back to the sermon, we see that Jesus unloads moral challenge after moral challenge onto his listeners. There isn't time to analyze the effect of each of the following statements, but each one seems to be the product of someone who is continually promoting the "radical" because it is ultimately the "sensible":

> "Do not store up for yourselves treasures on earth, where moth and rust consume and where thieves break in and steal; but store up for yourselves treasures in heaven, where neither moth nor rust consumes and where thieves do not break in and steal. For where your treasure is, there your heart will be also." (Matt 6:19–21)

> "No one can serve two masters; for a slave will either hate the one and love the other, or be devoted to the one and despise the other. You cannot serve God and wealth." (Matt 6:24)

"And can any of you by worrying add a single hour to your span of life?" (Matt 6:27)

"Strive first for the kingdom of God and his righteousness, and all these things will be given to you as well. So do not worry about tomorrow, for tomorrow will bring worries of its own. Today's trouble is enough for today." (Matt 6:33–34)

"You hypocrite, first take the log out of your own eye, and then you will see clearly to take the speck out of your neighbor's eye." (Matt 7:5)

"In everything *do to others as you would have them do to you*; for this is the law and the prophets." (Matt 7:12, emphasis added)

Of course, this last piece of teaching shows us what he meant when he said that he wasn't going to abolish the old Jewish law. He didn't mean he would be officious over every clause and subclause, but rather he would promote a wildly prodigious spirit of love, which could infiltrate all of our dealings with the people around us. We are still struggling to implement this simple principle every day of our lives!

This sermon is a masterwork. Some say it is a compendium, and that he didn't teach all those things in one sitting. Who cares? As a work of literature, it has fueled the bold and endless use of antithesis, simile, and metaphor in our literature at its finest. As a compendium of ethical guides, it is startling in its radicalism: it calls on us to live a way that we would never do if we only followed our natural instincts. However, it is also strangely mainstream and not radical at all: Who, looking at the tragedy of the world, has not at one time or another pondered how different things would be if we did even a modicum of what is recommended in this sermon?

Returning to the central idea and purpose of this book, the Sermon on the Mount does not make me like Jesus. Its overwhelming ethical vision helps me to believe that he is divine, and that makes me want to heed him; I want to see the world he envisions.

However, it doesn't make me like him. That's the honest truth. Maybe it doesn't need to.

CHAPTER 5

THE RULE BREAKER

After Jesus finished saying the Sermon on the Mount, a change occurred in the crowd who had gathered to listen, and there was also a change of strategy by him.

Matthew tells us, simply, that "the crowds were astounded at his teaching, for he taught them as one having authority, and not as their scribes" (Matt 7:28–29). The words of the sermon, so powerful on the page for us now, must have had an even greater impact on the ears of the listeners then. The imagery, the situations he describes, and the contrasts he makes—which were salt-and-pepper everyday analogies to the people of his day—made a strong connection with the people's lives. What he was saying made sense to them, pure and simple, and it was also startlingly fresh.

However, what was exhilarating to the first generation of listeners now seems like mainstream thinking to us. We've lived a further two thousand years with these teachings in the background, like the echo of the Big Bang that continues to pulse subliminally through the universe. Not that we've always implemented them, but we've called upon them when we've needed to correct our behavior: as cultures— the antislavery movement driven by the Christian principle, "Do unto others…"; as nations—Western peace movements have called upon Jesus' teaching of love for enemies; and as individuals. These teachings have made us who we are or, rather, the tension between them and our human nature has informed our intellectual and moral discourse.

The teachings are ingrained in our law, as evidenced whenever a judge employs his discretion and applies mercy.

As a general rule, we have wanted to do what Jesus taught, except when our blood is up and our human nature dominates us, which is most of the time. That's when we want to revert to revenge, judgment, greediness, and self-protection. That's the very time that Jesus seems remote and alien and his teachings seem to be impossible ideals; lunatic ravings. That's when we need to remember them and act upon them most; that's when they could do us the most good, and that's when they would actually make our lives better.

Let me recount a story. It's about the one time I did as Jesus taught and turned the other cheek. I was teaching in a school, and shared a classroom with a colleague. It was early in the arrangement, and one day when I walked into the classroom, I noticed that the desks were in a different order from normal. So I had the class reset them. I thought my colleague must not have had time to do so after some inventive lesson that had required the different arrangement. Little did I know what I had started! The next day, when I went in to teach in the same room, I found that my colleague had turned all the desks to face away from the board, to face, in fact, the blank back wall of the room, which rendered my lesson impossible. She was making a point, a rather unpleasant one: how dare you rearrange my seating plan! It was all a terrible misunderstanding; she had not yet realized that we were sharing the room long-term, and she had wanted her rearrangement of the desks to be the permanent setup. She saw my act of rearranging the desks as a sort of assault on her rights, and took revenge.

Of course, I was furious; furious at the act, but also furious that such a breach had occurred in a previously friendly and professional relationship. Why hadn't she just asked me about it? Her action seriously affected my lesson that day, and I had to reteach the lesson two days running because of the time it took to reset the room. I wanted to shout and scream, but for some strange reason, Jesus' words from the Sermon on the Mount came to me:

"If anyone strikes you on the right cheek, turn the other also."
(Matt 5:39)

Of course, it can be regarded as a metaphor, which means to offer no resistance to an enemy. At that moment, she was an enemy, and the worst kind; one who had been a good friend.

Who knows what had caused the behavior? It was not in keeping with her character. However, we are not asked to understand; we are asked to accept and forgive. Understanding may come later, but we can't wait for it before adopting Jesus' radical/sensible approach. I could have taken revenge and rearranged the room yet again. I could have gone to the principal, pretending collegial concern for the psychology of a colleague, while really dumping her in it—a glorious revenge!

For some reason—call it the Holy Spirit blowing where she may—I chose meekness, silence, a kind of loving response in the circumstances. And I waited.

It worked! Three days later, my colleague came to me quietly and said she was concerned that our previous relationship had been broken. I explained to her my point of view on the misunderstanding, and she explained hers. She was sorry for her behavior, and I was in no way wanting her to feel uncomfortable about it any further. We never spoke about it again; we didn't need to. Jesus' way of dealing with an affront worked. A human confrontation had been resolved peaceably.

I can only think that this is the kind of effect his words had on the crowd: his words had an authority that made people trust them and try his way; they must have found that his way worked. This may explain the very rapid spread of Christianity in its early days: it produced pleasing results.

As Matthew says, the crowd changed. However, Jesus also changed; at least, he changed his strategy. He no longer conducted mass healings, and when he did private ones, he did everything he could to discourage the gathering of unwieldy crowds. When he comes down from the mountain, he encounters a leper and heals him, and then he tells him not to spread word about the healing (see Matt 8). Jesus, it might be argued, had been too successful as a healer, and the crowds were unhelpful to his immediate mission. From now on and whenever possible, he would keep healings a quiet affair.

However, the stories of individual healings recounted to us by Matthew give us a warm insight into the personality that was Jesus. The first astonishing thing we see is that he cured a leper, the arch-outsider, considered a sinner by the sheer fact of his disease. Diana, Princess of Wales touched AIDS patients in recent times, as did Elizabeth Taylor, that woman with a heart of gold and every precious jewel! Jesus, having made his way to the center of society, started reaching out to the most outcast of outcasts.

He was beginning to break all the rules.

Jesus was a deliberate and sustained rule breaker. In fact, it was his most endearing quality. In chapter nine, he asks Matthew the tax collector to join his mission, and he goes and eats at his house. Tax collectors were even worse than lepers: they not only sinned by extorting more tax than was necessary to make their quota, they also managed to keep in perfect health, unlike the aforesaid!

> When the Pharisees saw this, they said to his disciples, "Why does your teacher eat with tax collectors and sinners?" (Matt 9:11)

The Pharisees, those self-appointed, self-righteous masters of the traditional law, criticized Jesus, undermining him on the grounds of mixing with "sinners." His reply is insouciant in the extreme: "Those who are well have no need of a physician....I have come to call not the righteous but sinners" (Matt 9:12, 13). The Pharisees keep up the campaign against him, so in chapter 11, he gets in another dig at their duplicity: "For John came neither eating nor drinking, and they say, 'He has a demon'; the Son of Man came eating and drinking, and they say, 'Look, a glutton and a drunkard, a friend of tax collectors and sinners!'" (Matt 11:18–19). To the modern sensibility, this mingling by Jesus with lepers, tax collectors, and "sinners" was as if he had chosen to eat with radio "shock jocks," Bernie Madoff (author of one of the most fraudulent Ponzi schemes in financial history) and, God forbid, Nicki Minaj!

The next big "no-no" Jesus commits is to do good work on a Sabbath. The Sabbath was the day of rest. You were not supposed to do any work. To give an indication of how important such a breach was, let me tell you about the Sabbath elevator. A few years back, I was fortunate to stay in New York with a good friend, who lived next to Mt. Sinai Hospital on Fifth Avenue on the Upper East Side (nice address!). Now and then, I would go in to the ground floor of the hospital to the cafeteria for breakfast. One of the great pleasures of life is sitting with a bowl of cereal and milk, reading the *New York Times*, and contemplating the joys of the day ahead in New York City—if you have money to pay for them!

Off the side of the lobby were the elevators, and next to one of them was a sign that read, "This is a Sabbath Day Elevator. On the Sabbath, it will stop at every floor without the need to push a button." This special service was a courtesy to orthodox Jews who could thus visit the sick without doing any physical work on the holy day of rest, even so much as pressing a single button.

Pretty strong religion, eh? And demanding a tower of discipline of its practitioners.

Nevertheless, Jesus cured a man with a shriveled hand on the Sabbath (see Matt 12). The Pharisees complained. How could he be a teacher of God's ways if he broke such an important rule and worked on the day of rest?

Jesus wiped away such inflexibility about the traditional Law when he said, "The Sabbath was made for man, not man for the Sabbath" (Mark 2:27). It's a terrific line. In it, he encapsulates a principle that has stayed with us till today. He isn't saying that we should be lawless, just sensible in any implementation of the law. For better or for worse, the difference between the more liberated culture of the West and other stricter legal religious cultures stems from this comment. No law should stand in the way of good works. In other words, the rules can be broken any time they stand in the way of love.

A few years ago, I organized an excursion of students to the city to see a production of Arthur Miller's play *The Crucible*. A large number of students were involved and they traveled together on the train to the theatre. On reaching our destination, it became clear that three students had not arrived with the rest. They turned up, but they turned up late. Two of them had gotten off the train halfway into town. They had done the wrong thing and were listed for a school detention the following week. However, in the intervening days, it became clear that they had gotten off the train because their friend, the third missing student, had missed the train at the very start, so they had decided to get off our train and meet up with her on the next one, so that she wouldn't have to come all the way into the big city alone.

Needless to say, their names were quickly removed from the detention list. The rules are made for people, not people for the rules! Or as St. Peter says, "Love covers a multitude of sins" (1 Pet 4:8).

This flexibility is also based on a common sense that eludes the powerful when they see their system of power threatened. The Pharisees and some "teachers of the law" ask Jesus (see Matt 15) why his disciples don't wash their hands before eating. Apparently, it was a ritual that was designed to make a man clean in a spiritual sense, not just for hygiene. In fact, the challengers are referring to the whole special way food was prepared by them, since they were, supposedly, spiritually superior beings. Jesus turns on them with his fiercest salvo yet, a war cry against hypocrisy. He points out that they manipulate the law in dreadful ways themselves, even to avoid spending money caring for their own parents; he quotes from Isaiah, "This people honors me with their lips,/but their hearts are far from me" (Matt 15:8); and then he does an uncharacteristic thing: he actually calls a crowd together for a specific teaching session aimed at embarrassing the guts out of his questioners.

> "Do you not see that whatever goes into the mouth enters the stomach, and goes out into the sewer? But what comes out of the mouth proceeds from the heart, and this is what defiles. For out of the heart come evil intentions, murder, adultery, fornication, theft, false witness, slander. These are what defile a person, but to eat with unwashed hands does not defile." (Matt 15:17–20)

Once again, Jesus rips up the rule book and gets to the heart of the matter. It's a shatteringly liberating principle. No longer will anyone be hidebound by finicky ethical procedures. The issue is no longer how you follow a certain ritual; it is the quality of the person's intentions that matter from now on. A person will be judged on their heart, their core, their inner self, and not on their outer actions. Outer actions can prove *false*; the true nature of the person will always remain *itself*. No doubt, this is why he tells us elsewhere not to judge another person a "sinner" for we can never really know. As King Duncan says in Shakespeare's *Macbeth*:

There's no art
to find the mind's construction in the face.*

For what it's worth, Shakespeare made virtually an entire career out of this one principle, for nearly all of his plays are about people who, in ways both tragic and comic, seem to be what they are not.

However, the most dramatic and the most history-changing way that Jesus breaks the rules is in his establishment of something the world had never seen before; something we have all grown so used to, that we fail to see its significance and undervalue it at our peril. Jesus broke every rule in the book when he created a nontribal, non-racial religion, a faith for every racial group, every culture, and every society on the planet.

This theme in his work begins innocuously. A Roman centurion, not a Jew—not one of his own *tribe*, so to speak—asks Jesus for help to cure his servant (see Matt 8). Jesus offers to come to his house, but the centurion declines, saying that Jesus could cure him from where they are standing: "Only speak the word, and my servant will be healed" (Matt 8:8). Jesus is genuinely impressed and complies immediately, saying, "Truly I tell you, in no one in Israel have I found such faith" (Matt 8:10). It is worth noting the warm-heartedness of the centurion. He is requesting help for a *servant, his social inferior*, and his language carries a rich sense of compassion: "Lord, my servant is lying at home paralyzed, in terrible distress" (Matt 8:6). This, too, would seem to have impressed Jesus. This is the first time Jesus' ministry reaches out beyond the Jewish tribes and embraces the "other," a Gentile.

The next time Jesus responds to a non-Jew also results in a healing, but the tone of the encounter could not be more different. In fact, at first reading Jesus comes across in a poor light. It's worth reading the whole episode:

> Jesus left that place and went away to the district of Tyre and Sidon. Just then a Canaanite woman from that region came out and started shouting, "Have mercy on me, Lord, Son of David; my daughter is tormented by a demon." But he did not

---

*William Shakespeare, *Macbeth*, Act One, Scene Four, Lines 11–14 (1.4, 11–14), Signet Classics, rev. ed. (April 1, 1998).

answer her at all. And his disciples came and urged him, saying, "Send her away, for she keeps shouting after us." He answered, "I was sent only to the lost sheep of the house of Israel." But she came and knelt before him, saying, "Lord, help me." He answered, "It is not fair to take the children's food and throw it to the dogs." She said, "Yes, Lord, yet even the dogs eat the crumbs that fall from their masters' table." Then Jesus answered her, "Woman, great is your faith! Let it be done for you as you wish." And her daughter was healed instantly. (Matt 15:21–28)

The story ends happily, but why is Jesus so grumpy at the start?

A key phrase at the start of the episode is "went away." Having encountered much opposition throughout his public teaching, Jesus goes to a distant region where he thinks he can have some rest. (Mark's Gospel actually mentions that he and his apostles were staying in a private house, and he didn't want to be disturbed.) So he's not on display, but this woman hears that a healer is in the vicinity and tracks him down. She pesters him, and he's tired. It's worth noting that Jesus does not reject her; at first he doesn't respond at all, but it's the disciples who want him to send her away. Jesus seems to be considering what to do in this particular circumstance. He rightly reminds the disciples that his mission is to the Jewish nation, so he was devoting his energies to building a team that was "in the know." After all, there was no Internet, no radio, no TV, and no mass communication to take a message easily across the nations. It's ridiculous to imagine one man, Jesus, being in any way able to spread his message widely as we do now; the result would have been dilution and exhaustion—and he was already exhausted!

Nonetheless, he lets the woman come to him, so there's something going on, something sub-textual in the exchange with the disciples that tells them not to stand in her way. There could be a touch of irony in his words, "I was sent only to the lost sheep of Israel." After all, this non-Jewish woman is invoking the Jewish title of the Messiah, "Son of David." Is she sincere? No one can be certain why Jesus tests her faith further; he may know something about her that is not apparent to us; it may be that, initially rebuffed, she needs to break through to a more solid understanding of the "bread" being offered.

Of course, many have argued that Jesus is being unnecessarily brutal here. The problem with that interpretation is that it runs against the rest of what we know of his personality. As I say, he may just have been humanly tired, and irritated if she weren't sincere. It's odd that she keeps screaming at him. Is she taunting him? She may be speaking from bitterness. This might explain the need to push her toward sincerity.

What is clear, however, is that once Jesus is satisfied—and his satisfaction may be that she has grown in appreciation of concepts necessary for her salvation; there's a deep subtext here—he wastes no time, as with the centurion: her daughter is already healed—salvation has come even to the Gentiles! These events foreshadow the time, after his incarnate mission on earth has ended, when his trained disciples will go out across the world to heal and convert all the Gentiles.

With the Roman centurion and the Canaanite woman, the door to a universal faith has been opened.

However, the strongest, although once again seemingly innocuous, breakthrough moment in the development of a nontribal religion is when Jesus is teaching a crowd and his family comes to interrupt him and bring him home.

> While he was still speaking to the crowds, his mother and his brothers were standing outside, wanting to speak to him. (Matt 12:46)

He responds to the crowd (and I don't sense the tone is necessarily aggressive): "Who is my mother, and who are my brothers?...For whoever does the will of my Father in heaven is my brother and sister and mother" (Matt 12:48, 50). More than any of the other moments of Jesus' rule-breaking, this is the clincher, because this breaks forever the stranglehold of family—and therefore tribal—loyalty, which can corrupt a sense of universal love, stand in the way of a shared faith for everyone, and prevent a relieving sense of unity with people of other races.

In one sense, there is not a single thing wrong with family loyalty, and there's an awful lot right about it: Family loyalty is the glue of society. The forces within a family are vital for raising children carefully, safely, and wisely; it takes a lot of energy! Through family, we have our first experience of love—we hope! In an enormous universe, we have familiar people around us who reassure us, even when they can be just a bit annoying.

I didn't know the importance of family until there was none around me. I spent a year teaching drama in North Carolina. To be cut off from my brothers, sisters, and mother was suddenly existentially exhausting. To be surrounded always by unfamiliar people is unnerving. You always have to strain because of the accent if you are in a foreign country, reactions are always slightly unexpected, there are differences in the meanings of some words, a different emotional history, and a different sense of humor. They don't know you and you don't know them; every social outing is a test-run, as if you're feeling the ground ahead with a stick in a minefield. Sometimes there is nothing better in life than to sit surrounded by those nearest and dearest—your family.

However, family loyalty can also be society's greatest problem, and to see what Jesus is getting at we have to divert a bit.

Alert! Alert! Digression ahead!—it's got a point about Jesus if you can wait long enough!

Did you ever see the British movie *Love Actually*? It was very well received and won several awards. I went to see it, and left after about ten minutes; its premise was wrong, wrong, wrong! In the opening, the camera panned across scenes of family reunions: fathers and sons, mothers and daughters, husbands and wives at Heathrow airport, and the voice-over of one of the characters—actually the British Prime Minister—was saying that the love we could see amongst those family members was "all around," that it was comforting in a hostile world to remember it, and implying that this was an unquestionable good.

While there's no doubt that that kind of love is all around, it is not necessarily an unquestionable good.

Think about it. There is a natural devotion of parents to children, because they are their offspring—their children are their genetic future. This leads to a natural preference for their children's well-being over that of other people's children. In wealthy societies, the dangers of this affection go largely unnoticed; perhaps there might be some disputes between parents on the sidelines of a football or soccer game if little Johnnie is unfairly penalized by the referee. Sometimes it gets a bit out of hand even in polite society. In 1991 in Texas, a mother, Wanda Holloway, attempted to hire a hit man to kill the mother of a girl who had been chosen instead of her own daughter for the school's cheerleading team! Even the hit man thought this was pretty poor behavior, and turned the murderous mother in. The effects of this genetic preferencing become more pronounced in desperate societies such as in some parts of drought-ravaged Africa, where food is scarce, and neighbors are sometimes forced to trample each other to catch food parcels off the backs of trucks for the sake of their own children. This is in no way to point the finger at Africans—my point is that if we were to take away the comforts of middle-class society, we would all behave in exactly the same way: our children; our "selfish gene" future—thank you, Richard Dawkins!—will always come first.

Families tend to build alliances with other families of like interests or needs. Soon, social networks and political parties grow from such naturally shared goals. In America, working-class families have traditionally congregated around the Democratic party. Small business families and families whose parents work in the world of large corporations have tended toward an affiliation with the Republican party. In England, it's the Labour and Conservative parties; in Australia, the Labor and Liberal parties, and so on. These groups develop sets of principles and ideals that can make us forget that really they are just congregations of families joined together by similar desires for their children's future.

In fact, whole nations are forged from family and tribal interests, which are joined together by geography to face shared challenges of survival. When these family and tribal interests are challenged by another nation, the countries go to war over such; they trample each other for the grand food parcel that is "territory" and "resources" in an entropic universe.

In short, I believe genetic favoritism—call it "genism"—ultimately causes the unrest we see on a grand scale in the world. In short, family ties and tribalism lead to war.

Now, we are often told that it is "religion" that causes wars. I think this is nonsense, at least when it comes to the major religions that have been around since Christianity. Wars have been launched by all kinds of people, religious and irreligious. In our own time, secular countries, that is, countries where governments don't represent religions, like America and England, have gone to war for such abstract ideas as "freedom" and "democracy." Religion itself hasn't *started* wars—unless we mean the religion of tribal pride, where the tribal god is only a collective emblem of the tribe's belief in its own superiority, and so becomes the symbol of the tribe's right to survive. George Bernard Shaw once wrote, "Patriotism is the conviction that this country is greater than all others because you were born in it." We all fool ourselves into believing that our tribe has a greater claim to survival than any other on account of some superior quality or belief on our part. I believe that if you strip away the rationalizations, you will always find the root cause of war is the simple desire for genetic survival of a nation or tribe and the natural rivalry of one tribe or nation against all others.

A few years ago there was a televised panel discussion that included the foreign ministers of Israel and the Palestinians. They both raised points about history and territory to justify their claims to the land of their forefathers, and of course disagreed with each other on many issues, but both agreed that peace was needed for the future of their children—but for the future of whose children? The conflict continues because the two sides have yet to agree for whose children peace is needed.

So what is the role of the rationalizations? In other words, why haven't we gone to war without feeling a need to justify it to the international community and ourselves? Why have we not been cynics, realists, or even nihilists when it comes to killing people who are "the other"? Psychologists would say that the rosy terms of rationalization have been necessary to resolve what is called "cognitive dissonance" in the collective mind of a warring nation. Let me explain. Cognitive dissonance is an uncomfortable feeling caused when one's actions are in conflict with one's conscience. Most of us most of the time go around with the thought in our heads that "I am a good person." However, at times of national conflict, we have been called upon to kill other people. How have soldiers, as well as the community at home who sends them forth, reconciled the two conflicting thoughts, "I am good" and "I have killed fathers/brothers/sons (even, nowadays, mothers and sisters and daughters)"?

There has been only one way to resolve the mental conflict. We have had to convince ourselves that our actions were for a "greater good." It hasn't been enough to say, "I did it for my family; for survival," because conscience reminds us that the other fellows have families too. We have had to convince ourselves that the other side—that whole tribe or nation—offended some deep ethical principle and threatened our way of life to such an extent that they forfeited their right to live.

Thus, rather than suffer the terrible anguish of extreme cognitive dissonance, we have justified killing in aggressive wars by saying we fought "for democracy," "for freedom," or "for God," in short, for a higher cause. Religion has not started wars—it has been part of a smorgasbord of useful rationalizations once conflict has started; but I believe the conflict has always had its roots in genetic or family survival.

Now, I've been using a lot of the present perfect tense: "rosy terms of rationalization *have been* necessary...," and so on. It is possible that such cognitive dissonance, caused by conscience, has been the product of two thousand years of Judeo-Christian history. Christians and Jews have an acute conscience in matters of killing both because of the Sixth Commandment and because of Jesus' comments about anger and aggression in the Sermon on the Mount. In contrast, ancient, pre-Christian despots boasted of slaughter. Take this, from the annals of the ancient Assyrian king, Sennacherib:

> In my third campaign I marched against Hatti, king of Sidon, whom the terror-inspiring glamour of my lordship had overwhelmed....I laid siege to (Hezekiah of Judah's) strong cities...and conquered them....I drove out 200,150 people, young and old, male and female...and considered them slaves....I imposed upon him...tribute...(including) his own daughter and concubines.... (*Annals of Sennacherib*, c. 700 BC)

If any monarch, premier, or president carried on with such sadistic boasting now, he'd be deemed the maverick leader of a rogue state! If one wishes to be a modern world leader, one must always justify murder by appealing to a higher cause and so satisfy international conscience. International conscience has been shaped mainly by precepts of Judaism and Christianity, those monotheistic "cousin" religions who both believe in one, ethical God. Furthermore, the United Nations has always resided in Christian countries and its underlying precepts are Judeo-Christian. If that weren't enough, Buddhism has as one of its central precepts, "Avoid killing or harming any living thing." Some other religions—not all—are similarly sensitive to the problem of killing in war. One dare not think what the world would be like if such a collective conscience were lost, and war needed no justification in an appeal to higher principles. How deep does a conscience go, if it be not highly aware of an ultimate divine judgment?

Remind me: What's this got to do with Jesus?

It's got a lot to do with Jesus. It's probably the thing a person nowadays could like him for most. Coming back to Jesus' words: "Who is my mother, and who are my brothers?…Whoever does the will of my Father in heaven is my brother and sister and mother." He establishes a new principle. Natural family affection is not to be regarded as superior to adherence to the principles of God. (If we want to know what those principles are, we must look back to the Sermon on the Mount and such teachings.) The consequence of this is extraordinary: birth into a particular tribe, race, or nation is no longer the basis for inclusion in the family of God. Faith and its consequent loving action toward *all* people is the glue of the new, spiritual "kingdom." Thus, Jesus has unlocked the door to the idea of an equal, universal, nonracial, nontribal, nongenetically favored community: a family of believers across the entire world; the end of "genism."

These words are the reason why, wherever you go, you find followers of Christ in every country, of every tribe and nationality. This is why, when a pope is installed, he might be from Italy, Poland, Germany, or Argentina. It's the reason why a Christian who falls from this universal regard for human equality and descends into being racist, regarding some humans as "other," does something deeply wrong that needs to be confessed, forgiven, and healed. It's also why this Jewish man called Jesus managed to reach out to all people, and why his Jewish followers changed a tribal religion into a global one. It's one of the most dramatic turning points in human history. It creates a new way of seeing our relationships with one another across the globe: we are not rivals, we are brothers and sisters. This vision was passed on to his followers including St. Paul, who spread it throughout Asia Minor and the Mediterranean region, and their converts carried it as far as it could go.

If the vision were made complete, it would immediately put an end to war. Short of some kind of psychological deficiency, it is very hard to kill your own brother or sister or mother. Furthermore, if the "other" becomes "your own," the necessary rationalizations grow much, much harder to invent!

It is also immensely disheartening. How can we ever match this vision that Jesus presents so clearly? Why are we still at each other's throats when we know it gets us nowhere? (*I'm not speaking of defensive war; I don't think there's any doubt that a Hitler must, sadly, be fought, and victory over him did get us somewhere, most definitely!*)

I hate the fact that Jesus inadvertently disheartens me, but I do love his vision. The great rule breaker breaks the greatest rule, the law of nature, and makes a nonracist, non-*genist* future possible for all humanity. We're not out of the woods yet. We've seen how terrible the world can be *with* the justifications and rationalizations, but forcing leaders to justify their aggression is slightly better than what came before, no question; and also better—if we lose sight of our spiritual, familial, and *universal* responsibility to each other that Jesus teaches— than what may follow.

CHAPTER 5 1/2

WHO IS EXCLUDED?

So, if this new faith is to be universal, is anyone excluded? Certainly! People who don't want to be included are excluded. They exclude themselves.

Jesus says, "People will be forgiven for every sin and blasphemy, but blasphemy against the Spirit will not be forgiven" (Matt 12:31). Not being forgiven by God is a kind of polite "code" for "you're out on your ear!" It's the line in the sand defining who's in and who's out. If you're interested in being in, you'll have to know what "blasphemy against the Spirit" is. However, before we even start on that, we should clarify what on earth is this Holy Spirit. Jesus talks frequently about it, so we'd better try to get some grasp of it, since it might be important in deciding whether or not we would like him.

The Holy Spirit is said to be the third "person" of the Creator. Like God the "Father" and God the "Son" (Jesus), the Holy Spirit is God. He created the world, as reported in the first book of the Old Testament, Genesis 1; he inspired the apostles at Pentecost, as told in the second chapter of the Acts of the Apostles; in chapter 8 of St. Paul's Letter to the Romans, he is an intercessor on our behalf with the Father; and he counsels us through our conscience. According to chapter 6 of St. Paul's First Letter to the Corinthians, our bodies, once converted to Christianity, are temples of the Holy Spirit. St. Paul also tells us that the effects the Holy Spirit produces in the believer are love, joy, peace, patience, kindness, goodness, faithfulness, gentleness, and self-control (see Gal 5). In other words, the Holy Spirit is the active agent of God's personality in this world.

(I know some of you must be thinking by now, "What is this? God is three people? What have you been drinking? Do they all share clothes?" I admit: believing in three "persons" in one God—the technical term is the Holy Trinity—was never a problem for me. If that sounds odd, I should explain I was a Doctor Who fan in my younger years; I grew up with the idea that a beloved, caring character who went about saving the universe could be found in three different forms—the magical William Hartnell, the delightful Patrick Troughton, and the most sophisticate of sophisticates Jon Pertwee. There was no doubt in my mind that they were all one "Doctor." So when the priest on Sunday spoke of God as three persons, I didn't even blink. [Then along came Tom Baker. But that's another story!] Other similes to explain the Trinity have included that of water, which appears as liquid, ice, and steam, but always remains H_2O; and even Neapolitan ice cream—chocolate, vanilla, and strawberry but all one gloriously united repast!)

So what is blasphemy, or sin, against the Holy Spirit?

To put it simply, it is the deliberate refusal to accept God's mercy and forgiveness. This may take the form of *despair*, ceasing to hope for personal salvation (the word *despair* has in it the idea of de-Spiriting oneself); it may take the form of *presumption*, that is, believing you can save yourself without the grace of God; it can be *impenitence*, which means resisting the work of the Holy Spirit in your life; *obstinacy*, which means persisting in a serious sin that you know is serious; *resisting divine truth*; and even *envy* in some circumstances.

I remember vividly an encounter with a boy when I was at school, back in 10th grade, when we must have both been about fifteen years old. This boy, whose name I have forgotten but definitely not the look on his face, was bullying another boy, whose name I remember but am happy to leave out so he may save face. I intervened, something that was uncharacteristically brave I assure you, but he wasn't a very big bully. The boy who had been bullied went away quickly; he wasn't going to hang around in case the culprit got another chance, and we were left there together, aggressor and interloper. The bullying was very verbal—the aggressor liked to find out a person's psychological weak spot and skewer it. I don't remember the words of the actual bullying itself, but I remember putting forth a fairly urgent idealistic statement about how we should treat each other better than he had treated the other boy; and I remember the final words of the bully to me, aimed at entirely flattening my idealism: "That's how the world *is*!" And that final word *is* was an accusation; he clearly thought I was a moron for thinking that any other system of behavior was possible apart from the law of the jungle. Furthermore, to his way of thinking, because that was the way the world *is*, he was justified in *knowingly* adding to the pain of it. There was no shame in his heart at being a bully. He simply *was what he was*, he was saying, as a bear is a bear or a cow is a steak.

As I think about that long ago episode again, a flutter in my stomach tells me that I partly believe his dark vision may be correct —bullying is all too common, at a personal level, between groups and classes in society, and among nations. It is sad to think that he thought that way, that his young life had already led him to such a hopeless conclusion. Maybe I'm making too much of it—after all, children tend to parrot what they've heard from their parents, so he may not have truly believed it himself.

Nevertheless, if he did believe it, I would have to conclude, unfortunately, that he had surrendered to despair and had already committed the sin against the Holy Spirit. This thought makes the memory of him very, very sad. I wonder what he's believing now.

Rejecting the Holy Spirit has to be a deliberate act of rejecting God, so it's not quite the same as rejecting membership of a certain church down the road. A lot of people have good reasons for not wanting to be part of a church. Experience can be an agonizing teacher and can make us fearful of people who offer seemingly magical solutions to all of life's troubles. Gee, it would be a horrible thing to be the cause of someone disliking the Church so much that the person rejects the Holy Spirit. However, it's also true that a lot of people reject their perception of the Church because they want a more authentic (in their eyes) experience of the Holy Spirit; they want to believe and they want to be inspired to do good; but they don't believe the Church will answer their desire. It can get fairly complicated, which is no doubt another reason why Jesus urged us not to judge!

People can lead good lives and do great things for their fellow humans after rejecting the Holy Spirit. After doing so, life can be reassuringly familiar and even comfortable; there are still enough good things in the world to enjoy life without the Holy Spirit. It's not a necessity for a comfortable life now. Hopkins, as we've seen, called life without the Spirit "Carrion Comfort"—the flesh can be satisfied and a person may be happy. Rejection of the Holy Spirit is not the same thing as sadness or lovelessness or misery.

Jesus is not being condemnatory in his comments about blasphemy against the Holy Spirit; he is simply stating a fact, more in sorrow than in anger: rejection of the Holy Spirit can't be forgiven by God because the person doing the rejecting doesn't believe in or want God's forgiveness. Fine! It's a free universe.

As we have noted, Jesus doesn't force himself on anyone and neither does the Holy Spirit, he tells us. You have to want what's on offer.

This sounds OK to me.

However, I do like St. Paul's list of the gifts of the Holy Spirit. I could get into that!

CHAPTER 6

THE KINGDOM OF HEAVEN IS LIKE…

Discussion about the kingdom of heaven doesn't do much for me. Matthew has a string of parables about the kingdom of heaven (see Matt 13), but I can't help feeling it's an anticlimax after the Sermon on the Mount. It's worth reading them all before moving on with this chapter.

What is the kingdom of heaven? Clearly from what Jesus says it is *a state of being* in *this* world first of all. It is not something that only begins beyond this world. It may stretch up to heaven, but what matters about it for us, when we first hear about it, can be experienced in the *here and now.*

We know this from the parables Jesus told about it. He says the message of the kingdom can be missed or even dismissed by some (the parable of the sower); people living in the kingdom still have to put up with bad influences all around them until the end of time (the parable of the weeds and the parable of the net); the kingdom starts small and grows into something enormous (the parables of the mustard seed and the yeast); and finally, the kingdom of heaven—this state of being—is something very, very precious, so much so that it is worth more than the combined riches of everything else a person possesses (the parables of the hidden treasure and the pearl).

It's clear that all these experiences of the kingdom are part of our life here on Earth.

It's also clear that we are to pray for this state of being to come into our lives; an idea that is expressed in the Lord's Prayer (*Thy kingdom come!*).

Beyond that there's not much more to say about it: the behaviors suggested in the Sermon on the Mount, in unison with the action of the Holy Spirit (love, joy, peace, patience, and so on) will move a person more and more into the kingdom. In speaking of John the Baptist, Jesus says, "Among those born of women no one has arisen greater than John the Baptist; yet the least in the kingdom of heaven is greater than he" (Matt 11:11).

From the parables of the mustard seed and the yeast, it seems that entering the kingdom is at first only a quantum leap, which really means a small shift; initially, conversion to Christianity is not so much monumental as instrumental. Clearly, however, that subtle change in a person's direction winds up changing everything in his or her life: priorities, affections, desires, actions, values, and the things they are willing to do and not do. It is as if a spiritual change starts at the molecular level and progressively overtakes the entire being.

It was essential for Jesus to provide a language, a set of images, so that we could crystallize his message. The phrase, *the kingdom of heaven*, is as powerful a metaphor as we can possibly have been given, and the similes he uses to characterize it are just as forceful. I'm grateful to him for that. Furthermore, the parables are exquisite literary creations, poetic essences, and marvelously authoritative as he reached for analogies in the daily experiences of his listeners to help them to understand. He was an effective teacher; has there ever been a better one?

CHAPTER 7

THE HUMAN SIDE OF JESUS

So far in the Gospel of Matthew, Jesus comes across as a profound teacher, a man with a message, a miraculous healer, a prophet, a wise man, and a role model. Too many such super-heroic impressions can become tedious and even, dare one say, repugnant. What of his simple human side? Is that likeable? We get a strong sense of this side of him toward the end of chapters 13 and 14. There are a few stories in these chapters that, taken together, have a gentle dramatic shape to them and work almost as a play-within-a-play—like an interlude with its own emotional structure and unified beginning, development, and conclusion.

Jesus goes back to his hometown, and his hometown responds dismissively. It's not that the people there don't see his powers; they do. They marvel at his great teaching and his miraculous healing abilities. The real problem for them is that he has gotten too big for his boots. Matthew tells us that they witness his greatness but "they took offense at him." In other words, the small-town boy who made good has injured their pride, so they reject him for emotional reasons, not logical ones. Jesus is forced to admit, "Prophets are not without honor except in their own country and in their own house" (Matt 13:57) and he goes on his way. His tone seems a little disappointed. We're used to thinking of God as being wrathful or merciful or loving; Jesus introduces us to a more human God, who can be melancholy.

Shortly after, Matthew tells us that the disciples of John the Baptist come and report to Jesus that John has finally been executed by King

Herod, and in striking circumstances. John has been in prison, and Herod has stayed his hand because John is highly regarded and he, Herod, doesn't want the people to hate him. Now, in a rash moment, in front of dinner guests, Herod has promised his step-daughter anything her heart desires, and she has requested John's head on a platter! As is often the case in Matthew's Gospel, pride is the culprit. Herod doesn't want to kill John, but he is ashamed to lose face in front of his honored guests.

When Jesus is told, Matthew recounts that "he withdrew from there in a boat to a deserted place by himself" (14:13). In other words, Jesus is grieving. His cousin—presumably his boyhood companion—has now died, and it comes as a double blow after the rejection by his hometown. It's as if the final vestiges of childhood are being taken from him, and it hurts Jesus like any other man. Who knows what other feelings were churning within him: perhaps he was thinking of Mary's cousin Elizabeth, who would be grieving too, as Mary, his mother, would one day have to grieve for him. A parent should never suffer the death of their child; perhaps he is thinking of that too. We can't help but feel sympathy for him at this point. So much is left unsaid, but the situation is painfully familiar to anyone who has lived a little time on this small planet: joyful memories of childhood would have flooded back and mingled with the painful realizations of maturity, like flotsam knocking together in the rapids.

Then what happens? A crowd follows him to the solitary place. That's all he needs, another bloody crowd! He has well and truly gone past the point at which he craved a crowd, especially when so many of the people in it would be latching on to him for misguided reasons.

What does he do? Tell them to go away? Turn his back and head further up the mountain? Matthew tells us "he had compassion for them and cured their sick" (14:14). This is a fine man. Compassion! It's an unusual word to be applied to God. It means to share the pain of someone else. That is what he does here. He feels their suffering with them. Jesus never turns his back on ordinary people and their trouble, but at this point in his life, he'd be forgiven for seeking a respite of some kind. Yet he does not. As we have seen, this same man can speak with such thorough wisdom; he is clever with smart, on-the-spot rejoinders when challenged; he articulates an extraordinary vision of a world united by membership of one spiritual family, and has the power to heal lives, not just illnesses—someone whose qualities are so astonishing that the word *divine* could be used to describe him, even by people who don't necessarily believe in some other-worldly god. This "divine" personality is moved, in this difficult moment, to be not only *human* but warmly *humane*.

In fact, his largesse increases. We've seen that at a certain point he didn't really want endless crowds constantly using up his time, and yet here, he not only heals and teaches, but *feeds* all of them. He even stays behind still greeting people and tells his apostles, who are themselves exhausted, to push off on a boat ahead of him. They cross the lake. Only when the last members of the crowd have left does he once again find a solitary place, this time up a mountainside, and, we are told, he "prays." I can't help suspecting it was a prayer of gratitude: gratitude for the crowd and their needs, which took him out of himself and reminded him that a sense of mission can overcome the paralysis of grief.

He now has to catch up to the apostles on the boat, and he does so in a rather spectacular way: he walks on the water—without a surfboard. Peter tries the same party trick and fails miserably: he starts to sink! Jesus, still on the water, rescues him. Matthew says, "Jesus *immediately* reached out his hand and caught him," (14:31, emphasis added) capturing another moment of humane tenderness, almost a reflex of compassion, even in the midst of the divinely miraculous: God on the water reaches down and grips the arm of the desperate mortal who, at that moment, symbolically represents all of us. What would have been the looks on both of their faces? Wide-eyed terror on Peter's part, slowly transmuting into incredulous relief; it doesn't take much to imagine, also, those tired eyes of Jesus, irritated at first, then beginning to light up with a brotherly smile—a smile that was restoring both savior and saved.

Then, after landing the boat on the other side of the lake, what do they find?

Another bloody crowd!

50

When they had crossed over, they came to land at Gennesaret. After the people of that place recognized him, they sent word throughout the region and brought all who were sick to him, and begged him that they might touch even the fringe of his cloak; and all who touched it were healed. (Matt 14:34–36)

These two chapters provide vignettes of the human Jesus—a warm-hearted God. He didn't want crowds, and he had just suffered two personal blows. The first crowd seems to have restored him. Having prayed, he has this moment of extraordinary divinity again, walking on water, transcending the very physical world that was home to the disappointing humans who had dealt him the blows, only to reach the other side, and become cheerfully resigned to the fact that he had a job to do. A job! By then, healing had become work, but he had always known what he could give people:

"Come to me, all you that are weary and are carrying heavy burdens, and I will give you rest. Take my yoke upon you, and learn from me; for I am gentle and humble in heart, and you will find rest for your souls. For my yoke is easy, and my burden is light." (Matt 11:28–30)

Light for them, maybe, but a bit of a drudge for him. However, he accepts it, even in the midst of personal grief and disappointment, and moves on.

What a man.

CHAPTER 8
JESUS AND CHILDREN

Nowadays, there is a tendency to suspect the worst of single men who want to hang around children, and there is even a shadow over fatherhood and the treatment of children by fathers, with fears of violence and incest and so on. A flood of bad news stories about child abuse has hardened our hearts. This is a tragedy of our times, both that stories of such abuse are ubiquitous and that we must even think such dark thoughts about men, who in most cases are entirely well-intentioned. We must pray to be healed from such darkness both real and imaginary.

Jesus' disciples wanted to protect their master from children who might pester him; he himself had to tell them to relax and let the children do as they liked. "Let the little children come to me, and do not stop them; for it is to such as these that the kingdom of heaven belongs" (Matt 19:14). It's a delightfully welcoming remark, but what on earth does it mean?

I don't think he meant that children were innocent, for two reasons. First, because they're not—children can be vicious, and they are definitely self-centered by the very nature of their neediness as infants and dependents; second, if he were saying that the innocent make up the kingdom of heaven, well, it contradicts everything he's been saying elsewhere about who actually enters the kingdom of heaven, because elsewhere the message is clearly different: sinners, prostitutes, tax collectors, gluttons, and drunkards can enter the kingdom so long as they have a repentant heart, and a repentant heart is not an innocent heart.

The (translated) phrase "to such" helps us to understand the meaning of the comment: "to such as these that the kingdom of heaven belongs." It is not the age of the children but their disposition that makes them a model for those who would join the kingdom: they are impulsive, enthusiastic, and trusting. Most children, unless they have been damaged by terrible experiences brought upon them by unkind adults, by their nature trust in their parents, are fearless, and love life. The analogy seems clear: we need to have childlike trust in a parent God, so much so that we step out in confidence, and thus have life and have it to the full. This is not the same thing as having materialistic possessions to the full.

Jesus is not being mystical or mysterious here, but is once again pointing out the obvious. We all know what it's like when we meet an adult who retains a joyful, childlike disposition—and that doesn't mean they're idiots! They are like a breath of fresh air. My collaborator in musical theatre writing, Allan McFadden, and I were once auditioning actresses for a part in an upcoming workshop of a show called *Laura*. A few very competent performers came and sang for us and read some lines—all fine actresses and singers. Then, a young woman entered the room and lit it up with her enthusiasm, zest, and sheer liveliness. Her name was Shannon Ashlyn. At first we thought, rather cynically, that she was trying to win us over, charm us into giving her the part. After all, that is the job of an actor or actress; to persuade, so nothing wrong there. She got the part alright, but in the months that followed—in rehearsals and the casual conversations we had with her—to our amazement her seemingly effortless enthusiasm, hopefulness, and joy never let up, nor was it so overstated that we grew tired of it, either. It was simply a part of her. Although she was a sophisticated, hardworking adult, her attraction lay in her ability to retain the light of a child into later years. When I think of these comments by Jesus, I think of people like Shannon Ashlyn—people who have an ability to go on trusting and relishing, like children fresh in the world.

It's that trust that has often been abused in what is, in many ways, a darkened world. The history of child slavery, child exploitation, and child sexual exploitation is horrendous. If ever one needed reminding that there is evil in this world, this appalling history will do it. In recent times, there's been an emphasis on the terrible breach of trust by clergymen; no more terrible than breaches of trust by members of a child's own family, but terrible and gut-wrenching without doubt. However, for those who think abusive authority figures might get away with it, and for those who think the civil law courts may not dish out enough penalty for such predators, Jesus has a fearsome warning for those who might draw children from God either by causing them despair through abuse or by misleading them in any way:

> "If any of you put a stumbling block before one of these little ones who believe in me, it would be better for you if a great millstone were fastened around your neck and you were drowned in the depth of the sea." (Matt 18:6)

Further, he tells a parable of a single lost sheep and of a shepherd who goes to great lengths to track him down and return him to the flock. He concludes:

> "So it is not the will of your Father in heaven that one of these little ones should be lost." (Matt 18:14)

Jesus' words about children are always affectionate. Note the following comment:

> "Whoever becomes humble like this child is the greatest in the kingdom of heaven." (Matt 18:4)

And:

> "Take care that you do not despise one of these little ones; for, I tell you, in heaven their angels continually see the face of my Father in heaven." (Matt 18:10)

According to Jesus, there's no doubt that children's vulnerability is set at a high price in the mind of God, and fierce penalties will be exacted spiritually for those who breach their trust.

It's actually a remarkable dimension to Jesus' personality that he makes so many comments about the beauty of the souls of children. He isn't some remote figure, so haughty that the chatter and horse-play of toddlers irritates or bores him. He isn't an elitist when it comes to age or maturity—the door is open to everyone. Well, at least everyone who can keep a touch of the child about them.

I definitely like this about Jesus. Most people like people who like children.

CHAPTER 9

FORGIVING SEVENTY TIMES SEVEN

Have you ever felt out of step with the people around you, as if you're not getting it, or getting them, and so you have to work harder to get on their wavelength?

A few years ago while visiting an aunt, I was able to stay overnight in a room at a Dominican priory in Canberra, which is Australia's capital city, a kind of Washington, DC, on sleeping pills. (No, that's cheap! It's a great place. I once found Canberra's night spot. I got there too late and found that it had closed at six.) At dinner that night, one of the Dominican fathers invited me to join the community for early morning prayers in the chapel; and I mean *really* early prayers, at 5:30 a.m. Since they were so kind to me, allowing me to stay for free and have a meal at their expense, of course I accepted the invitation—with dread. The following morning, before even the sun was up, the fathers were dotted around the pews facing the altar, and I knelt with them, except I made sure I was well at the back. They had their ritual prayers down to a T. I joined in with an occasional, slightly delayed "Amen" or "Hail Mary," always playing catch-up. Well, it didn't really matter if I got things a bit wrong, being out of the way and up the back.

Then, the pace quickened. At a prearranged point in the prayers, the ritual moved to the altar. The fathers all got up and marched to the front, and sat in chairs facing each other across the sanctuary around the altar. Feeling that I might be perceived to be rude if I didn't join them, and also egotistically wanting to show off that I could match them in devotion, I hurried up and took a seat, right in the middle of them on one side of the altar. There proceeded a scene that belongs in a movie starring Leslie Nielsen or the Three Stooges. For each part of the subsequent prayers, there were *actions* attached. On this line, they knelt; on that line, they turned right; on the word *Amen* they bowed. I looked like the comic who's been shoved on stage at the last minute to make up numbers in the kick line and doesn't know a single step of the choreography! When they took a bow, I turned right; when they turned left, I knelt. At one point, stretching out my arms when they were taking a bow, I managed to hit the one next to me in the eye. The worst thing for me was that I had no idea when this shambles would end. I was trapped, completely out of step, and must have been turning redder than a stop sign on the main street. Over breakfast was the final insult—smirks badly concealed behind napkins, break-out guffaws uncontrollably launching half-digested Corn Flakes across the tablecloth. The fathers were as polite as possible, but I could readily imagine their full-throated laughter after I had gone.

I always think of Jesus' apostle, Peter, as being out of step at every turn. He wanted so much to impress the master, and every time, he would only end up embarrassing himself. When Jesus said he was going to Jerusalem in order to be sacrificed, oh-so-loyal Peter said "No!"—well, you would, wouldn't you?—and he got told off for it and must have felt a proper fool. When Jesus predicted all the apostles would run out on him once he was arrested, Peter protested, and then went straight out and pretended during the whole trial that he'd never even met the prisoner. And, as we have seen in a previous chapter, he sank trying to walk across water like Jesus.

In chapter 18 of Matthew's Gospel, Jesus, that model of consistency, is back on his hobbyhorse about forgiving people who harm you. Peter comes to him and asks what he thinks will be an impressive question: If someone sins against him, how many times should he forgive him? "As many as seven times?" You can imagine Peter practically waiting to receive a congratulatory pat on the noggin. Once again, he is well and truly out of step. Jesus says to Peter, "Not seven times, but, I tell you, seventy-seven times" (Matt 18:22); in other words, an infinite number. In fact, there's a joke happening here: to Jewish people "seven" connoted something complete, something thorough, because

God was able to rest from completing Creation on the seventh day; so "seventy times seven times" would be mind-blowing. Poor Peter! Jesus then proceeds to tell a story about a servant who owes his master some money. The master absolves the servant of the debt, and the grateful servant goes out and happens to bump into another servant, further down the totem pole, who owes him some money. He berates the debtor unrelentingly, having forgotten his own recent state of grace, and demands instant payment. The master hears about this episode, calls him back, and punishes him terribly.

Forgiveness is serious business in Jesus' teaching. He forgave Peter every time he was out of step. As we shall see, Jesus even did some forgiving on the cross, of the people who were putting him to death.

That's consistency.

All this forgiving and being forgiven, as far as I can see, is simply a way of acknowledging the reality of our earthly condition. It's like a verb with a very regular conjugation: I mess up, you mess up, they mess up, and we all mess up. It's life! Sometimes we mess up inadvertently; sometimes it's an act of malice; and sometimes sheer tiredness or hypoglycemia is all it takes to snap, to argue, or to lash out. After all, we are organic creatures in a material world. Everything we are, everything we do, and even our best intentions come under the sway of nature's rhythms. I don't know why—in fact, nobody knows why—but the world, which is full of good things and in which we can imagine and aspire to great things, is limited in its goodness. I often think it's the mere entropic nature of the universe, the fact that it takes more energy to create order than to let things slide, which makes life the way it is: as a result of this inbuilt natural paradox, we now and then fail and fall away from our highest moral goals, or the brain fails and we mess up without deliberation. Of course, it's a fair question to ask, why did God create such an imperfect world in the first place? Whichever way we answer the question, we are left with the problem of evil—not just moral evil, but also a kind of natural evil, whereby nature stymies us in all kinds of ways. Although there is no complete answer to the question (and it's worth reading the Book of Job in the Old Testament to see someone demand answers from God concerning the tragedy of life, and not get them), there is one tiny glimmer of an answer that rings true to me. St. Paul writes in his letter to the

Christians living in ancient Rome: "We also boast in our sufferings, knowing that suffering produces endurance, and endurance produces character, and character produces hope" (Rom 5:3–4). It is interesting that we could not be who we are—our character—without the troubles we have overcome. In some ways, the more troubles we have—"the weariness, the fever and the fret," to quote the poet, John Keats*—the stronger and more interesting the personality we develop. I suppose that if we didn't suffer much, we'd become like those stereotypes of insouciant aristocrats we often see lampooned in the movies—living waxworks with no spark of the individual in us at all—practically Botoxed to death!

Whatever the reason, we are surrounded by fallible humans, and we all have to put up with one another's frailty, both moral and natural. We can choose to respond to the hurts done to us with rage, outrage, and revenge, or we can choose to forgive. The first approach suggests a level of self-righteous pride that declares, with ferocious volume, "I refuse to be treated this way by the condition of the world! I am a superior being!" which places the speaker outside of the reality as experienced by the entire human population since the beginning of time. The path of forgiveness, on the other hand, does seem more sociable and realistic about human limitations. It isn't cowardice, and it isn't given without being requested; there's no point in forgiving someone while he's still laying into you without regret! Although, Jesus does just that—forgive his persecutors from the cross, unbidden. *Hmm...* So there's the choice: an endless cycle of injured pride leading to revenge, or the more peaceful method of acknowledging universal human weakness, which leads to mercy and reconciliation.

In which world would you prefer to live?

Meanwhile, I'm especially glad he forgave Peter.

---

* John Keats, "Ode to a Nightingale."

CHAPTER 10

THE LAST AND THE FIRST

Sometimes my children drive me crazy. They race up the stairs to beat each other to the front door, and the winner cries out, "I'm the champion!" I loathe such competitiveness, possibly because I'm no good at it. I often find myself saying to them, echoing Jesus, "The first shall be last and the last shall be first." I must say this comment fits my personality to a T. When I was a child, my own mother used to urge me to push myself forward in shops so that I would be served faster, rather than hold back for others to go ahead of me. I couldn't help it; there were an inordinate number of little old ladies in the local population of downtown Wollstonecraft where we lived, and they frequented the shops prodigiously, and I didn't want to be like George Costanza in *Seinfeld*, who would happily trample grandmothers if it were of advantage to himself.

I don't recall when I first knew that Jesus said, "The first shall be last and the last shall be first," but it certainly helped when they put me into the Under 13 H football team at school, a team so untalented that we always covered ourselves in ignominy. In the Under 13 Hs it was a dangerous business being passed the ball. Normally, glory awaits the holder of that leather bladder called a football, and the person who scores while possessing it is a hero. However, on that team, to hold the ball or to be anywhere near it was to be a hapless target. I quickly worked out that, due to a mysterious inherent reticence on my part, known in the trade as "incompetence," there was no way I would ever break through the opposing team and put the ball across the line, so my only option was to pay off the boy inside of my position—I was on the "wing"—to *not* pass me the ball. It cost me a lot of Kit Kats, Mars Bars, and other assorted chocolates that year. Fortunately, the following season relief came in the innovation, new to that school and I think to the world, of an activity known as "Winter Tennis," which, sport wise, was the last refuge of the desperate. Our tennis coach was even less interested in achieving sporting glory than we were, leaping into his car and driving off at the first merciful drop of rain, calling out over his rapidly receding shoulder, "Don't forget to pack up the racquets, boys!" We were the lame, the halt, and the blind, that band of winter tennis players, but the coach saw in me a kind of super-phenomenon of sporting incapacity. I couldn't even throw a tennis ball up in the air and hit it to start the game off (I think they call it "serving"). Hence, nobody wanted me as either partner or opponent. So, with a plainly conspiratorial wink, the coach banished me to the squash courts for what he called "private practice," by which he meant that if I disappeared, changed out of my sneakers into going-home uniform, and quietly quit the campus, he'd never come to check. In that school, there was a hierarchy: rowing, football, cricket, tennis, tiddlywinks, reading the newspaper, racing snails, and then winter tennis. Ah, yes! I took great solace in the thought, "The first shall be last and the last shall be first."

Jesus is very consistent about this idea. When a rich young man comes and asks him what "good thing" he must do to "get eternal life" (see Matt 19), Jesus tells him that if he wants to "be perfect," he must sell all his possessions and give to the poor so that he will have "treasure in heaven." The rich young man goes away sad, because he owned so much. He was a leader in material possessions; Jesus invited him to come follow him. In other words, this first among men had to humble himself and become last. It's interesting that this young man was sad when he heard Jesus' advice. It's as if he knew exactly what he stood to gain by entering this new faith, but simply couldn't conform his will to his wishes. In the rich young man we find again the tragedy of Faustus: a person who understands exactly what is right, but is incapable of doing it.

After this episode, Jesus tells his followers that "it is easier for a camel to go through the eye of a needle than for someone who is rich to enter the kingdom of God" (Matt 19:24). Jesus' followers fear that salvation is impossible; the demands just seem too hard for human nature to accommodate. Jesus reassures them, "For mortals it [salvation] is impossible, but for God all things are possible" (19:26). He's an interesting character: always setting the bar so high, and then immediately lowering it again. One minute it's as if you'd need to be an Olympic athlete of virtue—"the first"—to qualify, and then he turns around and says, don't worry, because God is running the event and welcomes all comers. It's probably the reason that he was so popular with such a diversity of people. For once, they could feel God loved them more than he wanted to judge them.

Still on the same theme, Jesus told a parable about casual workers in a vineyard (see Matt 20). Some come and start work early. Some turn up at the last hour of the day. The master pays them all the same wage. The ones who came first grumble about how unfair it is, but the master protests that he has the right to be equally generous to all workers if he so chooses. The last and the first were equals to him. (It's probably best not to think how the vineyard fared financially once word got around of this unorthodox method of payment!)

Later in the same chapter, a mother makes a typical motherly request to Jesus. She wants her two sons to sit by his right and his left side in heaven, positions of very high honor. Jesus refuses to answer, and instructs the disciples:

> "You know that the rulers of the Gentiles lord it over them, and their great ones are tyrants over them. It will not be so among you; but whoever wishes to be great among you must be your servant, and whoever wishes to be first among you must be your slave; just as the Son of Man came not to be served but to serve, and to give his life a ransom for many." (Matt 20:25–28)

In this episode, Jesus makes the point that the places of honor—up close to him on the right- or left-hand side—are reserved for a special kind of follower: leaders who serve and sacrifice themselves for their fellow human beings. The first shall be last and the last shall be first.

Then in chapter 22, he tells the parable in which a man is staging a lavish wedding banquet. When many of the village's leading people dismiss the invitation, he goes out and brings in strangers and poor people from the streets to fill up the places at the tables. The first are last and the last are put first.

It is a consistent teaching: *equality, service,* and *humility*—putting others ahead of you. It's also known as unselfishness, but that word is a trifle overused, even if its meaning is tremendously under-practiced.

It's an interesting idea. How would the world be if political, social, and economic leaders believed themselves to be, and behaved as, servants and put themselves last? I understand Bill Gates, the founder of Microsoft, is doing just that, vowing to give away a fortune before he passes on. Dick Smith, the famed Australian business tycoon and explorer, is renowned for his generosity. Andrew Forrest, a mining magnate also from Australia, is pioneering a worldwide campaign against child slavery. The man elected to papal office in 2013, Pope Francis, has chosen to live not in the papal suite, but in the hostel where visiting priests stay, and he has devoted his papacy to the betterment of the poor. These people are practicing the words of Jesus; putting themselves last so that others more in need can come first. When we hear of such action, it warms the heart.

It's a difficult teaching. Pride is powerful. We all chafe at the idea of bowing down. Only if we have a strong sense of the generosity of the Holy Spirit can we actually be prepared to surrender our own selfish desires and devote ourselves to the needs of strangers; otherwise we would feel that we were idiots to forgo the pleasures of this world. It is interesting that the American super heroes, Superman, Batman, and so on, each had a "treasury" to back up their work on behalf of humanity. Bruce Wayne had a fortune, Clark Kent had the ability to fly, bend steel, and see through walls, and so on. True, they had the disposition to do good works, but they also had the resources to accomplish it.

We all need a treasury upon which to draw. The saints, such as Mother Teresa, also have a treasury—that "treasure in heaven" of which Jesus speaks; an assurance of abundant life to come in paradise. Such an assurance would overcome the natural fear of stepping out as well as the tendency to hoard self-satisfaction. However, it isn't easy to step out in faith and put ourselves last. Wealth alone will not give us the confidence to do it. Wealth can be a stone that presses down our better selves; it can be a wall of fog consuming us, making us forever look inward rather than outward. Jesus is not making it easy here. He's not watering down the message in order to make friends. He's holding up a mirror, and making us see where our hearts truly lie, and we may not like what we see.

Just ask that sad, rich young man.

CHAPTER 11

A FEW THINGS ABOUT MARRIAGE

Oh damn, it's the marriage chapter! I was dreading this topic. Were you?

Marriage is the big personal issue of our time; perhaps of all time. After the Romantic poets came along, we aligned marriage with the idea of personal emotional fulfilment, and so now we face great potential for a kind of existential disappointment. Nowadays, young people in the Western world have more experience of failed marriages around them—it frightens them.

Additionally, people who believe most in marriage tend to suffer the most when relationships go wrong. I once knew a work colleague who told a horrible story: She had married with enthusiasm and hope as a believing Christian, but her husband turned out to be a user, who was emotionally withdrawn and physically abusive. She found she couldn't trust him, practically from the start. Toward the end of the relationship, she wound up going over to her parents' place after work each day. When she felt sleepy, she would drive home and go to bed. She simply couldn't face being in the same house with him a second longer than was absolutely necessary. It is hard to think of a situation worse than having to return home each day or night to a loveless, indeed hate-filled, marriage. We invest so much of our identity and pride into our choice of lifelong partner that to be met with such disappointment can be destructive of the inner spiritual life. My colleague held out as long as possible; she believed 100 percent in the sanctity of marriage. (The problem is that it definitely takes *two* to tango.) She tried everything: marriage counseling and even trial separation—always with a view of returning. Finally, flying in the face of everything she had believed in from youth, she filed for divorce. He refused to sign the papers! Only after protracted, dispiriting efforts to persuade him to do so did she find the peace she needed. Needless to say, her experience of such disappointment is all too common.

Wouldn't it be great if we could solve all the mysteries of marriage from the words of Jesus captured in Matthew's Gospel? Alas, it ain't gonna happen! Throughout the New Testament, there is a theology of marriage, but in Matthew we find Jesus responding to two main questions: the first about divorce, and the second about marriage in the afterlife. The first group of comments is hard to take now, but surprisingly, they were hard to take then too.

As recorded in chapter 19, some Pharisees come up "to test him" by asking: "Is it lawful for a man to divorce his wife for any cause?" (v. 3).

We live in a time of no-fault divorce, but even so, for the reasons of natural human pride mentioned above, people still feel an obligation, at least socially if not legally, to give strong reasons why they want to divorce. The question by the Pharisees might take us by surprise if we think of the ancient Jewish world as being stitched up and conservative, but if our divorce laws are liberal, theirs were positively anarchic. Imagine being able to file for a divorce for "any cause"! I'm thinking that this sounds great for the men, but what about the women? Divorce would have been a sure route to poverty for them, unless they were able to remarry.

The key to understanding Jesus' response lies in the three words that introduce the passage: "to test him." The Pharisees aren't sincere. They don't want instruction; they're not seeking pearls of wisdom to make them more loving people; they are not interested in changing their behavior as a result of his words to them. They are asking about the traditional laws, and they want an answer that will make Jesus out to be the opponent of Moses, in whose name the laws of Jewish society were drafted. It's a trap!

What does he do? He cuts through the legal issues—as he often does—and goes deep to the essence of the question: marriage is a fundamental state desired by God for his creation.

"Have you not read that the one who made them at the beginning 'made them male and female,' and said, 'For this reason a man shall leave his father and mother and be joined to his wife, and the two shall become one flesh'? So they are no longer two, but one flesh. Therefore what God has joined together, let no one separate." (Matt 19:4–6)

I don't know about you, but I recoil when I think of this comment in relation to abusive marriages—like the one outlined at the start of this chapter; but to be fair to him, Jesus isn't really talking about that aspect of marriage here. He's been asked a specific question to which he's giving a specific answer. He's simply saying that there is a deep, natural, and God-intended goodness in men and women forming permanent relationships. This shouldn't really surprise us. It reflects reality, doesn't it? There is something about romantic love that calls forth a desire for eternal unity and makes us want to promise ourselves to another person for life. We need to temper this feeling with a sense of willed commitment so that we don't just tumble at the behest of hormones into a terrible mistake, but the fact remains: human love encourages promises of "forever and aye." Furthermore, because human children require a particularly lengthy period of support—lengthier than your average eaglet, calf, or kitten—it is natural for humans to connect romantic love with a need for durability. Conversely, an entire history of "morning after" jokes depends upon the irony that the warm desire for eternal love the night before can be quite exploded with the dawn; and the anger of many a jilted man or woman comes from a sense of such profound human commitment rakishly betrayed.

Not only do we start by feeling a desire to love the *other* person for life; equally, there is in us a sense that *we* deserve a lifelong love. We are worth that; so we believe. Many a cynic will pooh-pooh the idea and roll his eyes and say, "I'll take love as it comes," but I'll go out on a limb here and suggest that, short of some kind of pathology, the cynic is merely protecting himself out of hurt pride. It is my view that if you scratch a cynic you will find someone desperately wanting to be loved and painfully desiring to love—for life! Am I wrong or am I wrong?

Furthermore, it is human to expect that love so strong will be affirmed by a strong statement of commitment, more binding even than a promise—a *vow*, and after we put our heart and soul into a vow, we can't help feeling terribly cheated if the other person does likewise and then breaks his or her word. To repeat, each of us is worth a lifelong love; one of the worst pains in life is to be denied it; and the greatest pain, arguably, is to have it only then to have it *betrayed*. This is why divorce is always a tragedy, and divorcees know that best. It can be a tumultuous tragedy or a quiet one, but the crack in the heart remains the same in any case.

Now, the same Jesus that shows boundless compassion for social outcasts, the poor, and the sick throughout his preaching ministry is not likely to turn around at this point and impose law for law's sake upon people in abusive and painful marriages. There's nothing in what he says here that is encouraging women or men to stay in that kind of relationship.

What he really is doing is battling one particularly insidious form of marital abuse, namely the dumping of the woman when the man is no longer attracted to her. Simple as that! The Pharisees are seeking approval for husbands to be able to abandon their wives on a whim— "for any cause." (*This reminds me of Hollywood star Mickey Rooney's famous comment, after having gone through eight marriages: "Always get married in the morning. That way, if it doesn't work out, you haven't wasted a whole day!"*)

> [Jesus] said to them, "It was because you were so hard-hearted that Moses allowed you to divorce your wives, but from the beginning it was not so. And I say to you, whoever divorces his wife, except for unchastity, and marries another commits adultery." (Matt 19:8–9)

Jesus is reinstating the sacred duty of the marriage vow and reminding them not to be shallow about important commitments you make in life. The qualification he makes—"except for unchastity"—has been a much debated subject. It may refer to the wife's fornication prior to marriage, that is, if she's found to have not been a virgin on the marriage night, allowing the husband the right to divorce her prior to final vows in the same way Joseph was tempted to break off his betrothal to Mary when it was found that she was with child. The suggestion is that the woman may not be committed to this marriage because she is in love with someone else. However, the exact interpretation of that phrase continues to be debated, and may have many interpretations, so we may as well move on.

Now, the disciples are present and when they hear this teaching, say to Jesus: "If such is the case of a man with his wife, it is better not to marry" (Matt 19:10).

Such a reaction is natural. The hearts were still hard. They are hard today. They always will be without the compassionating (to invent a word!) influence of the Holy Spirit. Marriage doesn't float about as a thing separate from the essentials of changed Christian behavior: it needs mercy, compassion, and kindness like every other part of our lives. In fact, you could argue that those things are needed in even greater supply in what is the *central relationship* of a person's life. However, just like the Pharisees who asked the question, the disciples aren't thinking about changing their values at a deep level the way Jesus is implying; they just wanted an out; they wanted the freedom to play the field. It's why Jesus spoke earlier of lustful thoughts as already being a form of adultery; he knew he was dealing with hard-hearted and selfish men on all fronts, who were in need of swift and repeated metaphorical kicks to bring their immoral thoughts into line! The disciples' reaction tells us that they were no saints. They were ordinary men who were keen on the status quo, which was heavily slanted toward the rights of men to dispense with women like broken toys. Jesus is not presenting anything radical or even overly burdensome. He is simply reminding the people of the sincere obligation of marriage, given the strong commitment and emotional need that are the marks of normal human love, as even our hard hearts deep down know only too well. Again, without this obligation it would be the women of the time who would have suffered more.

The next big encounter regarding marriage may not interest you. The Sadducees, a group of people who didn't believe in the resurrection, come and ask him about marriage in the resurrection. Sure, it sounds like a contradiction. It also sounds like another trap. Like the Pharisees, they wanted to trip Jesus up. Once again the impression is that these powerful men saw marriage as a game, not a commitment. Nonetheless, they pose him a neat legalistic conundrum:

> "Teacher, Moses said, 'If a man dies childless, his brother shall marry the widow, and raise up children for his brother.' Now there were seven brothers among us; the first married, and died childless, leaving the widow to his brother. The second did the same, so also the third, down to the seventh. Last of all, the woman herself died. In the resurrection, then, whose wife of the seven will she be? For all of them had married her." (Matt 22:24–28)

Resisting the temptation to say, "I'd have that woman investigated if I were you," he replies:

> "You are wrong, because you know neither the scriptures nor the power of God. For in the resurrection they neither marry nor are given in marriage, but are like angels in heaven. And as for the resurrection of the dead, have you not read what was said to you by God, 'I am the God of Abraham, the God of Isaac, and the God of Jacob'? He is God not of the dead, but of the living." (Matt 22:29–32)

Two big knockout punches here. First, he tells them bluntly that there is no marriage in heaven. Well, this is rather obvious. Why would there be a need for reproduction in heaven, or the care of children, or even sexual desire? (Does this mean that there is no reunion of loved ones? Not at all; it's a separate question.) If the afterlife is anything like it's often presented, there would be a form of bliss that would not require earthly versions of the same thing. There would also be no jealousy, so the brothers won't be arguing over possession of a woman. However, the second punch goes to the heart of the Sadducees' beliefs. We've already worked out that they were not interested in the question of marital fidelity, per se; they were using this question to ridicule Jesus' teachings about the resurrection. Having blasted their assumptions about marriage, Jesus goes on to tell them that the patriarchs—Abraham, Isaac, and Jacob—are still alive, and still in relationship with God. In other words, Sadducees, you're wrong! So stop bothering me with your silly tricks. Both his assurance and his logic impress the people: "When the crowd heard it, they were astounded at his teaching" (Matt 22:33).

Marriage and lifelong love by any name is of critical concern to anyone calling him- or herself human. In Matthew's Gospel, Jesus concentrates on marriage only when questioned about it by men wanting to undermine his broader claims of being the mouthpiece of God. We can look elsewhere across the other Gospels and the remainder of the New Testament to find all the strands of Christian teaching about marriage, but we shouldn't forget that the central tenets of Jesus' teaching remain the same for all human relationships, including marriage: mercy, compassion, and kindness; the things we all desire and value.

CHAPTER 12

THE GREATEST COMMANDMENT

In Matthew 22, a Pharisee asks Jesus, "Teacher, which commandment in the law is the greatest?" and he replies, "'You shall love the Lord your God with all your heart, and with all your soul, and with all your mind.' This is the greatest and first commandment. And a second is like it: 'You shall love your neighbor as yourself.' On these two commandments hang all the law and the prophets" (vv. 36–40).

Now, as already noted, the Pharisees as a group were inimical to Jesus' message, because their power depended on their exalted position in the religious culture, and Jesus was saying that there was no exalted status in religion. The Pharisee's question here is yet one more trap, which Matthew tells us plainly before the questioner begins.

How is it a trap? It's the old "damned-if-you-do, damned-if-you-don't" scenario. As soon as Jesus identifies one commandment, they'll get him for neglecting some other. It's a standard trick beloved these days by the sales- and ratings-hungry media: The president gives a speech about human rights, and the next day the headline reads, "President neglects childcare"; or the prime minister focuses on urban renewal, and the papers declare, "Prime Minister ignores health," and so on.

An important aspect about Jesus that we have learned on this walk through Matthew's Gospel is that he can think on his feet much faster than his would-be persecutors. They never get the better of him and by now you'd think they would have given up trying. He knows the motive behind the approach these people make; he understands the plan; and so, in characteristic style, he goes to the nub, the core, the heart. The Pharisee wants to talk law; Jesus talks love.

He isn't rejecting the traditional Jewish Law; Jesus is not interested in destroying a culture that has provided the groundwork for his impending sacrifice. He is simply reminding his accusers that the Law is in fact a guide to love. He cleverly quotes directly from Moses. The Pharisee is floored!

Hold on! We can't move on from this episode without breaking every rule in the book—*Get your breathing equipment on!* We're going outside Matthew for a moment! The cleverest thing Jesus ever said—and arguably the most compassionate and the most merciful—appears in *John's* Gospel. It's so spectacular that we have to go there now! (*You'll see why in a moment.*)

You've probably heard the story of when the Pharisees dragged out a woman caught in the act of adultery and dumped her in front of Jesus and said: "Teacher, this woman was caught in the very act of committing adultery. Now in the law Moses commanded us to stone such women. Now what do you say?" (John 8:4–5).

At first, Jesus didn't reply, but sat down on the ground and wrote something in the sand. So they badgered him some more. Holding stones, they were ready to execute the woman. The master of suspense, Alfred Hitchcock, in more than eighty movies and TV shows, never created such a heart-stopping, tense moment! This was for real—a life hung in the balance.

Jesus broke his silence and said quietly, "Let anyone among you who is without sin be the first to throw a stone at her" (John 8:7).

In my view, this is not only the cleverest thing *Jesus* ever said, it's probably the cleverest thing *anyone* has ever said in the history of the universe! Furthermore, it worked. John tells us, "When they heard it, they went away, one by one, beginning with the elders" (8:9).

However, the story doesn't end there. The woman remained with Jesus. Remember that she's an adulterer. Jesus stood up and said to her, "Woman, where are they? Has no one condemned you?" She said, "No one, sir." And Jesus said, "Neither do I condemn you. Go your way, and from now on do not sin again" (John 8:10–11).

Do you see why we had to go there? It's the same kind of challenge Jesus keeps facing in the Gospel of Matthew—a trap, based on traditional Mosaic Law. Once again, as so often, the challengers are not actually interested in learning the truth about how to behave; they only want to expose Jesus as the enemy of Jewish religion and society. However, John's story is even more dramatic than Matthew's accounts of such conflicts, because what Jesus says will not only win or lose a legalistic point, it will save a life.

The other reason we needed to hear the story is that it's a perfect illustration of Jesus' law of love—the law that permeates Matthew's Gospel. "Love your neighbor as yourself." He doesn't waste time arguing details of law, either about stoning or adultery or about anything else; to love God is not to be a pedant. To love your neighbor is to do what *needs* doing for him or her *right now*, and the law can go hang! "'Love the Lord your God with all your heart, and with all your soul, and with all your mind.' This is the greatest and first commandment. And a second is like it: 'You shall love your neighbor as yourself.' On these two commandments hang all the law and the prophets" (Matt 22:37–40).

That's the essence of Matthew's Gospel, and actually any part of the New Testament. However, I hate the fact that Jesus said that these were the greatest commandments. I deeply resent the call for me to surrender all my other interests to my love of God and neighbor. All my heart? All my soul? All my mind? I want to have *some* time to myself. Oh, I'm happy to go to church on Sunday and pay my dues, and even throw a few coins on the plate, but give me the rest of the week for my passions. I really don't want to give God everything, and I really don't want to care for my neighbor as much as I care about myself. It's all so terribly inconvenient. Why did he have to say it?

I don't like it at all!

CHAPTER 13

GOING FOR THE JUGULAR

Whom did Jesus hate? Am I allowed to say that: "Jesus hate"? Doesn't Jesus—doesn't God—love everyone?

In Matthew 23, Jesus goes on the attack targeting the "hypocrites."

First, it's worth clarifying who is a hypocrite. For Jesus, a hypocrite is not simply a person who preaches one thing and does the opposite. Everybody from time to time preaches one thing and does the opposite: the strict environmental campaigner who one night lazily leaves the lights on and burns up more coal; the ever-gentle humanist who respects humans, but one day gets so fed up and frustrated that he lashes out and slaps one; the reformed, pious teetotaler who succumbs to temptation and has a sudden, urgent drink; and don't we all honk the horn at the driver who does exactly what we did yesterday? We all occasionally fail to live up to our own standard. As St. Paul says, "All have fallen short...." In other words, a hypocrite is not your garden-variety sinner who keeps trying to do the right thing but every so often does the wrong one. We would all be hypocrites if the word referred to that sort of person—and perhaps, secretly, we all are a little bit. After all, the heart shifts ground very quickly to justify our own mistakes, and when it does, it is ever-so-briefly prepared, by corollary, to condemn the same mistakes done by others—a hypocritical double-standard, even if it only lasts a moment.

However, the hypocrites whom Jesus condemns (and he condemns them strongly!) are a much grander lot, and much more established in a sustained duplicity. The word *hypocrite* derives from the

Greek word meaning "actor," and it carries a certain sense of being a professional; being proficient in deception. The people he collectively loathed, the ones against whom he launched this tirade are the religious leaders who falsely presented themselves as models of godly behavior, who set the godly regulations to which the society was supposed to adhere, and who regularly condemned ordinary folk as spiritually inferior for not being able to live up to their own high standards. The hypocrites of whom Jesus speaks are the conspicuously religious and upright who, in private, didn't so much cringe at their own secret shames as laugh at their ability to pull the wool over the public's eyes. In fact, they are those people whose public utterances are so often and so much in contrast with their private behavior that they have no shame, and in some sense, no soul.

Hypocrisy is also not a static thing: one can become more hypocritical or less with time. As one's awareness of the complexity of life's moral challenges grows, one's youthful judgmentalism should shrink. In the story from John's Gospel that we noted in the last chapter, in which Jesus saves the life of the woman caught in the act of adultery, it is the elders who first retreat when Jesus says, "Let anyone among you who is without sin be the first to throw a stone at her" (John 8:7). The young ones have a greater capacity to keep believing in their own moral superiority. Over time, it grows harder to sustain duplicity in public, and the old often just don't have the energy to keep it up! However, over time it is equally possible for a hypocrite to add to his or her own hypocrisy by denying the self-truths that time exposes— for example, one's own laziness, lustfulness, or greed. We all have a responsibility to adapt our respect for others in the light of the growing awareness of our own weaknesses.

Furthermore, hypocrisy represents a lack of respect. Jesus respected people whom the hypocrites called sinners. He respected them enough to spend time with them; to go to their parties and to make public displays of honoring them, such as Zacchaeus, the otherwise hated tax collector whom Jesus openly befriended in the middle of a crowd one day. He respected them enough to challenge their weaknesses, but like the woman caught in the act of adultery, he did not condemn them, because he knew their hearts; he knew their circumstances and why they had responded to them in less than ideal ways, and he also knew if they were genuine in their desire to be reformed. In this regard, we should be grateful that we have a God who walked amongst us and knew what it was like to live in the flesh. If Jesus is a divine judge, he is one who has come to understand first-hand how hard it is to be a consistently good human.

To summarize, the people he condemns are not "sinners," but hypocrites, that is, people who deny their own sin while pointing it out in others, and continue to do so relentlessly. His most savage words are reserved for them:

"Woe to you, scribes and Pharisees, hypocrites! For you lock people out of the kingdom of heaven. For you do not go in yourselves, and when others are going in, you stop them." (Matt 23:13–14)

"Woe to you, blind guides!" (Matt 23:16)

"You…have neglected the weightier matters of the law: justice and mercy and faith….You strain out a gnat but swallow a camel!" (Matt 23:23, 24)

"You clean the outside of the cup and of the plate, but inside they are full of greed and self-indulgence." (Matt 23:25)

"You are like whitewashed tombs, which on the outside look beautiful, but inside they are full of the bones of the dead and of all kinds of filth." (Matt 23:27)

"You snakes, you brood of vipers! How can you escape being sentenced to hell?" (Matt 23:33)

To which the modern wit would say, "Jesus, why don't you tell us what you *really* think."

His ferociousness begs the question, why is hypocrisy the one sin that gets him riled? (He also got mad at the buyers and sellers who abused the sacred space around the temple in Jerusalem, but if you think about it, they were being hypocritical too.) It takes a lot to make

Jesus angry. We've seen him say that the one sin that cannot be for-given is the sin against the Holy Spirit, the sin of despair, but he does not become enflamed by the thought of it; his tone there is compas-sionate. He rescues from stoning a woman caught in adultery, and calms her down with forgiving words. He looks out on sinful crowds and feels mostly sorry for them and feeds them. In stark contrast, when he contemplates hypocrisy, he hurls more fiery epithets than a football fan does toward members of the opposing team. Why? I think it's because all those other sins are being done by people who have a sense of humility and realism: the sinner is willing to confront a truth that can open their hearts to loving others. They are learning respect for shared humanity in all its weakness. Those other sins allow growth of soul and soulfulness. Hypocrisy, as he says above, shuts the door in the face of others. It is entirely and profoundly selfish. It is a self-isolating sin, made the worse by its cynical belief in one's own ivory-tower superiority. However, it is not a superiority of morality, but rather a secret, self-destructive relish in one's own cleverness, that convinces one that there is no need of God's or, for that matter, humanity's truth.

Does Jesus hate the person who is the hypocrite? No. It is impos-sible to hate a person who is a hypocrite for the simple reason that the hypocrite is not a person. In ancient times, actors—that is, *profes-sional* hypocrites—wore masks when performing roles. For the period of the performance, the actor was not a real person. He was the mask, and he wore it not to conceal, but to reveal; in particular, to reveal the truth of the soul of a human character he was playing. In contrast, the hypocrite, by making himself a mask in real life, loses his soul, and so takes himself beyond the possibility of a true relationship with God or neighbor. Thus, the hypocrite also fails in the greatest commandment of all, for in order to love anyone, one must at the very least be *real*.

We get to know a person by learning what he or she loves and what he or she hates. When we consider everyone to whom Jesus demonstrates love, and then we see his fury at the one thing he hates, everything about him becomes integral and starts to make sense: the compassion for people who admit that they face real behavioral prob-lems; his moral realism in the face of sinners who are genuine about becoming free from whatever weakness is dragging them down; his sensitivity to people who have been condemned by a self-righteous elite; his reluctance to condemn anyone, and his readiness to embrace everyone who is *real*.

Certainly, Jesus begins to make sense and look very attractive!

CHAPTER 14

POLITICS AND RELIGION

In about AD 33, two thousand years ago, Jesus was arrested by authorities in ancient Judea, put on trial, and executed. On the third day after his execution, he rose from the dead.

Jesus died as a result of a familiar concoction of religion and politics. In fact, the motives of his accusers are so familiar that Matthew doesn't bother to go into them very much. The duplicity of the religious conspirators is best illustrated by a conversation they have with Jesus about taxes. The Pharisees, who dominated the religious culture of Jerusalem, "plotted to entrap him in what he said" (Matt 22:15). This is how Matthew records the conversation:

> "Teacher, we know that you are sincere, and teach the way of God in accordance with truth, and show deference to no one; for you do not regard people with partiality. Tell us, then, what you think. Is it lawful to pay taxes to the emperor, or not?" But Jesus, aware of their malice, said, "Why are you putting me to the test, you hypocrites?" (Matt 22:16–18)

Sound familiar?

It is sad that, while evil people not only recognize goodness and can even understand what it involves, they just can't bring themselves to do it. This group of Pharisees understands perfectly Jesus' integrity, his devotion to truth, and his resistance to bribery and influence: "We know that you are sincere, and teach the way of God in accordance with truth." If we want to know why they are so committed to remov-ing him, we need look no further. Jesus is building a popular following based upon the force of truth, not the power of social and religious status. He directly threatens their moribund, corrupted system and their duplicitous way of behaving. It is the common story of power and its attendant jealousy.

However, this isn't the only reason that he again calls them "hyp-ocrites." The fact is that the Pharisees couldn't care less about paying taxes to the emperor, or in other words, to the Roman authorities. They despise the Romans. The emperor and his governor are foreign, pagan sinners, and hateful to the very soul of Judaism. Jesus knows that the only reason they are asking him this pedantic question is because they hope he will either condemn himself under Roman law by teach-ing people not to pay taxes, or, if he unequivocally advocates obedi-ence to Roman law, he will alienate those of his followers who want their Messiah, their Savior, to be a political revolutionary. This is cer-tainly another trap.

In Matthew's telling of the story, Jesus says,

"Show me the coin used for the tax." And they brought him a denarius. Then he said to them, "Whose head is this, and whose title?" They answered, "The emperor's." Then he said to them, "Give therefore to the emperor the things that are the emperor's, and to God the things that are God's." (22:19–21)

Stymied, the Pharisees retreat to fight another day.

How often are we approached by smiling assassins like these, pouring forth devious flattery, and only wanting our ruin? Start a list sometime and see how long it is. This is the behavior that made Jesus hate hypocrites, because, as God, he could never have a relationship of love with men of straw.

The charges they finally get him on are his threat to tear down the temple and rebuild it in three days (a symbolic comment he made about his own body—a kind of temple, a sacred space of God—being crucified and being resurrected on the third day), and his claim to be the Son of God, or God himself in other words. From the point of view of the religious leadership of the day, these are serious charges without question, but there's a bit of regular old political theatre going on as well. When Jesus is asked by the high priest if he is the Son of God, he replies in the affirmative; this infuriates the high priest who dramatically tears his own clothes when he hears Jesus' declaration. Jesus would most likely have been unimpressed by somebody he regarded as a hypocrite tearing his outer garments. Don't forget that these are the people who made a point of wearing clothes specifically designed to display their piety. In fact, this conspicuous act of being scandalized is all show; we know the leadership has been trying to trap Jesus for months, so any feeling of scandal would by now have been very old.

This carrying on tells us something about the level of Jesus' following at the time he was arrested. It must have been substantial enough to be a real threat to the Pharisees and the high priest; their reaction is as much an expression of their personal fears of approaching irrelevancy as it is a piece of political showmanship. Jesus' methods for spreading the new faith seem to have worked: He chose to enter *into* people's lives rather than lead them out into the desert, so his ideas had infiltrated the center of society rather than nibbled at its fringes; his metaphors had been taken from daily life, so that his message was understandable by people without intricate knowledge of traditional legal and moral precepts; his topics were pertinent, so the people who listened felt that he spoke "with authority"; and finally, his healings substantiated his claims of being divine, so even those who were not exactly salvation minded nonetheless had turned to him as a source of hope. So the religious leaders didn't have the option to dismiss him as a crank; they could feel a seismic shift happening in the narrative of their own religion, and they were being left behind as the story was being hijacked.

Having established that Jesus has committed blasphemy (that is, an insult to God) under Jewish law, the Sanhedrin (the Jewish religious council) carted Jesus off to the Roman governor for capital punishment. Why? Judea at the time was a Roman province controlled by the Roman Empire. Some say that the Roman administration had declared that it did not want executions carried out by locals, that they themselves would supervise the legal deaths of criminals. In John's Gospel, the Jewish religious leaders, when asked by the Roman governor why they had brought Jesus to him, say by way of explanation that they "have no law to put a man to death." Really? Tell that to the poor woman they were eager to stone to death just to trap Jesus in a legal argument over Mosaic tradition! Blasphemy, breaking the Sabbath or not keeping the Sabbath, adultery, and rebellious children all warranted death by stoning. The religious leaders didn't seem to mind the possibility of getting their hands bloody on those occasions, so why not now?

The possible reason is that, since they first plotted to kill Jesus, he had built up an even greater popular following, one that was too dangerous to enflame. The evidence of Matthew points to a steady, sturdy, progressive increase in the crowds following Jesus in Galilee, and even in Samaria. Now the movement had reached Jerusalem, the religious center, and was clearly catching on at an alarming rate even there. Therefore, it was far better strategically to shift responsibility for Jesus' death to the foreign imperial power—Rome had a garrison of soldiers in every major town, including Jerusalem, and could handle any mob who wanted to rebel over his crucifixion.

However, it was a tricky political path to negotiate. The Romans, as far as we can tell, preferred to remain aloof in local religious disputes. Years later, around AD 112, in the Roman province of Bithynia, a Roman governor, Pliny, did all he could to avoid executing Christians merely on the basis of their religious beliefs. We know this because he wrote a letter to the emperor, Trajan, seeking advice on how to cool the tensions in his bailiwick without making religious martyrs of the Christians. Similarly, in AD 33, in the Roman province of Judea, Pontius Pilate couldn't have cared less about a minor dispute over Jewish theology and conflicting views of the locals about God. *Big deal! Pass me another grape!*

This partly explains why Pilate was so slow to take action. Further, he would have been wildly suspicious about the motives of the high priests bringing the matter to him in the first place, and would have seen that he was being set up to take the rap. To get a complete picture of these momentous events, we once again need to step outside Matthew briefly for some details. According to the Gospel of John, the religious leaders try to corner Pilate politically and make him take the desired action. They push the line that Jesus had claimed to be a king (remember all his parables about the kingdom of heaven?). Piously they declare, "We have no king but the emperor" (John 19:15). Ah, such devotion to the Roman emperor from these pillars of ortho-doxy! What fine acting! What they are saying to Pilate in effect is that Jesus was committing treason, not blasphemy; and treason, which con-sisted of any challenge to the emperor's majesty, that is, his supremacy, was a readily executable crime under Roman law. (Now we fully understand how they had tried to trap Jesus over not paying taxes to Caesar—they already had this Roman offense in mind as a way of get-ting rid of him.) Once a public accusation of treason was made, Pilate was forced to act. The governor would be open to censure in the imperial Roman court if he were to fail to take the necessary steps against someone claiming to hold greater power than the emperor. These religious leaders are no Romantics; they don't bother with ide-alistic or religious arguments in front of the pragmatic Roman official. They get Jesus on whatever they can: so Jesus is to be crucified not for blasphemy against God under Jewish religious law, but for treason against Rome under Roman civil legislation. *What a neat trick.* The spirit of Machiavelli was alive and well in the hearts and minds of the religious leaders in Roman Judea fifteen hundred years before Machiavelli himself was!

However, just in case you're thinking I may be anti-Jewish here—as indeed Western European Christian society was for two thousand years after these events—not a bit of it. Jesus and all his followers were Jews too. The issue is not Jewishness. The issue is power, and how powerful men behave to maintain their own power and crush all those who with good intent dare to threaten them. When political survival is at stake, how quickly the minds of the elite spin to find an ultimate solution! The threatened Sanhedrin and the cornered Roman governor do not make strange bedfellows in this marriage of convenience.

Forgetting for a moment the politico-legal shenanigans, it's interest-ing to ponder the Roman governor Pontius Pilate's personal take on all this. In Matthew's Gospel, Pilate is less of a personality than he is in John's account. There is less written of him. However, the real man must have had his own reasons for going along with the Jewish priests' desire. He couldn't have been a fool and reach the position he held; mastery of an entire Roman province. He would have deduced fairly quickly that Jesus wasn't claiming to be an earthly king but rather was a spiritual leader. It would have rapidly been clear to Pilate that Jesus' message was not one of violent sedition. Jesus' followers do not show up outside the governor's headquarters throwing rocks and threatening to torch the place. Furthermore, according to Matthew, Pilate knew that "it was out of jealousy that they had handed him over" (27:18).

From ancient history we know that the best thing that a provincial governor from Rome could do was keep the peace in the provinces so that taxes could be collected and the empire would be enriched. One of the reasons, for example, that the wealthy Roman Marcus Crassus joined the famous First Triumvirate with Pompey the Great and Julius Caesar was because he wanted a rebate for tax collectors who had been unable to do the annual collection in certain provinces due to civil disruption. The financial convenience of peace was the goal of any Roman governor who wanted his career to prosper.

So Pilate first and foremost is doing his Roman job, and doing himself some good too. The people are stirred up about something. How to stop the pot from boiling? Simple—put out the fire; to put out the fire, remove the kindling, and in this case, the kindling is Jesus. Removing Jesus is so straightforward a political mechanism that Matthew wastes no ink explaining it.

However, if we can understand the behavior of the persecutors, can we fathom the mind of Jesus during his arraignment and execution?

Jesus does very little. His silence and his few utterances make for powerful reading. It's an astonishing turnaround: the loquacious bull, the master teacher, the stylish proclaimer of the great Sermon on the Mount, becomes a dumb ox. When Pilate asks him, "Are you the king of the Jews?" Jesus replies simply, "You say so" (Matt 27:11). In context, this answer is so absurdly disingenuous that Pilate at first proceeds to find ways to let Jesus off; he knows Jesus is speaking spiritually or at the very least metaphorically. In a way, Jesus' reluctance to protest his innocence speaks of his innocence—too much bluster would invite suspicion. Jesus seems resigned, not as a perpetrator, but rather as someone who knows too well how the system works and naturally expects the worst of it.

If Jesus were simply human, his stoicism would invite admiration: he is Socrates accepting the hemlock of life without quibble. However, being God as well as a man, his acquiescence is more than resignation: it is a monumental act of love, because it is an overwhelming act of restraint. This divine forbearance, if that is what it is, is exceptional when one looks at the gross detail:

> Then the soldiers of the governor took Jesus into the governor's headquarters, and they gathered the whole cohort around him. They stripped him and put a scarlet robe on him, and after twisting some thorns into a crown, they put it on his head. They put a reed in his right hand and knelt before him and mocked him, saying, "Hail, King of the Jews!" They spat on him, and took the reed and struck him on the head. (Matt 27:27–30)

Maybe you saw the film about Jesus' passion produced by Mel Gibson. Critics complained it was a gore fest. It was. I saw some of it; much of the time, I looked away. In some ways I thought the movie was a poor one, but its depiction of the actual torture of Jesus had the grossness of authenticity. This mockery of his claims to kingship, this brutal attempt at emotional and mental degradation, reminds us of what human nature is capable of when it lacks the Holy Spirit. In a culture reduced to a mean equation of winners and losers, winners have no sanction against their relentless need to assert mastery over the vanquished. There is no evidence of any redeeming humanism in these soldiers, and their added viciousness is also fueled by racism: Romans were the greater race, Jesus was just a Jew.

Ironically, if we accept that Jesus is the divine and sinless being history claims, he is in the act of saving the souls of the evil men whom he allowed to torture and execute him. The complexity of this situation is the most likely reason he remains silent. It makes sense. How could he ever explain this to these people? They are beyond the attractive power of truth, the light of reason, or any thirst for justice. They are merely the people who make this world miserable, and they protect themselves as much as possible from the misery they make by barriers of ill-gained comfort, even if it is only the comfort of escaping the degradation they have visited upon others. One of Jesus' regular catchphrases: "Let anyone with ears listen!" never sounded more ironic than when one considers the moral deafness of these soldiers and their superiors.

So there are two large silences in Matthew surrounding the crucifixion of Jesus: one concerning the painfully obvious and boringly familiar motivations of the politico-religious conspirators in the affair, and the other born of a loving vision that soared beyond the undignified pettiness that will always be the preserve of souls that are merely political and only religious.

The Roman soldiers took Jesus to a nearby hill outside Jerusalem and executed him by hammering him in an awkward position to a wooden cross. His death, by asphyxiation and blood loss, took about six hours (see Matt 27). During that time, ghoulish observers relentlessly hurled insults and mockery at him; in true human fashion, they kicked a man while he was down. There's nothing unusual in that, for that's what we're like. That's what we do. That's what we always do. It makes us feel "good." When the toppled Iraqi dictator Saddam Hussein was executed in 2006, reports were deliberately released to the effect that he was taunted to the very last second of his earthly life by the soldiers commissioned to carry out the act. It was as if some people wanted to revel in vengeful fashion at his mortal despair. Some may say it was justified. Such behavior certainly wasn't justified in the case of Jesus, and such behavior will never be justified. (*On a side note, even though I would never cheer for the Spanish Inquisition, it is interesting that that grossly punitive arm of the medieval and renaissance Catholic Church would employ a band of comforters to accompany a heretic to the stake where he was to be burned, urging him up to the last moment to repent of his sins, the aim being to save a soul, not crush it into despair—a very different approach, although it's hard, given the horrible context, to call it a Christian one either!*)

In contrast to the typical, the familiar, the human, and the vile, Jesus prayed to the Father in heaven to forgive his tormentors: "Father, forgive them; for they do not know what they are doing" (Luke 23:34). (While this detail comes from Luke's Gospel, it's in keeping with everything Matthew tells us about the character of the man.) We may speculate on the complex theological questions involved in the crucifixion of Jesus, such as the way in which these men's evil is employed by God to bring about a good, namely the saving of humanity, but before that we should simply take time to respond with a sadness deeper than a well to the unjust death of a *genius of love*; whose only "crime" was wanting to democratize God and to free people from the slavery of a hypocritical religious elite that offered them nothing at all in the way of mercy, hope, or joy.

As one contemplates the corrupt situation involved and, by contrast, the Man who was lifted horribly and beautifully above it, such a response goes far beyond mere liking.

CHAPTER 15

THE DISLIKABLE JESUS

Judas did not like Jesus, and I for one like the reason he did not like Jesus. Judas was the man who identified Jesus to the men who were sent to arrest him. Judas had made an arrangement with the chief priests and was paid "thirty pieces of silver" to lead a group of men to Jesus in order to capture him. This event was on Passover after the Last Supper Jesus had shared with the twelve apostles. Judas's betrayal is possibly the most famous one in history, closely followed by Marcus Brutus's betrayal of Julius Caesar.

Why did Judas betray a man who the apostles believed was the Messiah, the Savior of Israel?

We know the tipping point. It was when a woman poured expensive perfume on Jesus' head at the home of Simon the Leper (*nice name!*) in Bethany, a town about half a day's walk from Jerusalem. Putting perfume on somebody's head was a common practice then, a mark of respect and affection for a guest in the house. The disciples were angry and objected to the amount of the perfume used as well as its high cost, because the money could have been used for the poor. Straight after this event, which took place two days before the fatal Passover when Jesus was captured and put on trial, Judas went to the chief priests and made the deal: "What will you give me if I betray him to you?" (Matt 26:15).

It is worth paying careful attention to the incident of the expensive perfume, which may have driven Judas to action against the man he had "given up everything" to follow. Interestingly, the other apostles were also scandalized; by accepting the woman's gift, Jesus incensed his most loyal followers.

> Now while Jesus was at Bethany in the house of Simon the Leper, a woman came to him with an alabaster jar of very costly ointment, and she poured it on his head as he sat at the table. But when the disciples saw it, they were angry and said, "Why this waste? For this ointment could have been sold for a large sum, and the money given to the poor." But Jesus, aware of this, said to them, "Why do you trouble the woman? She has performed a good service for me. For you always have the poor with you, but you will not always have me. By pouring this ointment on my body she has prepared me for burial. Truly I tell you, wherever this good news is proclaimed in the whole world, what she has done will be told in remembrance of her." (Matt 26:6–13)

What's going on here? The disciples gang up on this woman. Forget the fact that Jesus has often been feted by wealthy patrons. Forget the fact that he once turned six enormous jars of water into wine and that he could make a fortune for the poor any time. Forget that he once sent the loaves and fish market into a spin by feeding five thousand, gratis! When a woman gives him an expensive gift, well, they think, there's got to be something wrong! So there's a definite male bullishness—indeed, there is bullying—taking place. The woman is an easy victim.

In typical fashion, Jesus leaps to her defense, and in fact puts the disciples' masculine self-righteousness back in its box by telling them that this woman will be remembered throughout history. (What *male* from Alexander to Caesar has not longed for such an accolade?) He completely disempowers their attack on the woman.

Furthermore, and it's a relief for us, Jesus legitimizes the innocent giving of gifts between acquaintances even in the face of worldwide poverty. Although according to theology he is here to rescue the macrocosm, he understands the need for humans to express their love and affection in microcosms across the world. Once again, he recognizes that circumstances and occasions have a variety of priorities.

The kingdom of heaven is not, in this sense, monolithic or one-size-fits-all. He legitimizes a commonsense approach to gift-giving between friends while not advocating complacency; a continuing duty to the poor, which he himself acted upon repeatedly, is implied. It's just that you shouldn't fret over doing something nice to someone once in a while by giving them a treat.

However, the fact remains that the disciples protested, and they protested in thoroughly reasonable terms. They protested from a principle, and a good one. Had it not been Jesus who told the rich young man to sell all he owned and give the proceeds to the poor? The teaching then seemed clear, and it fitted the messianic model: he spoke like a champion of the rights of the downtrodden against the wicked and wealthy overlords. Then, he'd sounded like the Messiah; now, he has once again befuddled them.

Well, we know he did that a lot. We know that he didn't meet their messianic expectations; he wasn't a worldly leader, he was an unearthly one. Right at that moment, this woman's self-esteem was being hammered by the disciples; that was the injustice at hand, and Jesus wasn't going to stand a bar of it! Possibly for Judas, this tiny act was confirmation; it was the last straw. Jesus was misleading the people and had to be stopped.

What do we make of Judas? He is clearly a highly principled man, a chosen disciple, believes in all the right things, and is devoted to the poor! So why did he go from being a follower to being a betrayer? People generally carry within them the seeds of surprising choices for a long time before they break open. Judas, a good man, seems to have harbored ambition for revolutionary change, a change in the circumstances of this world; specifically, a change for the better for the Jewish race. (If the devil had tempted Judas with "all the kingdoms of the world" as he had Jesus, how would Judas have responded?) Perhaps it was the very fact that Jesus wanted spiritual change first and social change second that disillusioned Judas. He was a young man in a hurry, as the saying goes, and when he saw that his ultimate hopes for the poor were being stymied, the elastic that had permitted him to indulge Jesus snapped back from its full extension. He had to turn to the high priests then; there was no other source of security he could think of. It was his duty to stop this false Messiah.

WOULD I *LIKE* JESUS?

Certainly, there was all that righteousness in Judas, but there was also the fact that Jesus' rebuke to the disciples over the matter of the expensive perfume may have been a particularly hard blow to Judas's pride, given that he was so highly principled; and I suspect that his reaction, running to the authorities, was as much driven by sheer resentment as it was by those high principles. Nonetheless, in Judas's case, it was primarily his form of goodness, not his evil, that made him come to dislike Jesus.

In the midst of this most "dislikable" action by Jesus, there is actually another astonishing dimension: this Lord, this King, this God permits his followers to challenge him, and they, who have known him best over three years, *still* feel completely comfortable doing so! Can you imagine an Adolf Hitler, a Joseph Stalin, or a Saddam Hussein permitting such flagrant dissent? Remember those maudlin conferences of Saddam Hussein's where his cabinet sat around the table silent, cowering? This scene is nothing like that. This suggests a mutual respect. Jesus the master is also Jesus the loving listener. To an extent, the event has the quality of a bit of a disagreement between "mates." (This might be the Australian in me, who sees it in such a way!) Jesus actually engages with the dissenters, he actually welcomes their critique, and he does not punish them. Why would he? They've spoken from love, just as this woman acted from love; he respectfully accepts both the disciples' censure and her care. What some see as the most shocking of Jesus' actions—accepting expensive perfume that could have been sold for the poor—may actually be one of his kindest.

The other dislikable thing about Jesus is that he has too much love to offer us. *Too much love.* Too much love is distasteful; it tends to invite its own rejection. It's as if his love is a burden too heavy for the beloved to stand. G. K. Chesterton, the great Catholic writer of the early twentieth century, wrote of "the furious love of God." Admittedly, he was speaking of it in a most unusual context—passing by fireworks after a conversation with a devil worshipper! However, there is something of that incendiary energy of pyrotechnics in the love expressed by Jesus. To prove his love, he seems willing to do anything, go anywhere, into any house, into any conversation with friends, foes, philosophical debaters, searchers, doubters, Samaritans, and Gentiles; he comes ready to heal anyone who asks; he grabs metaphors, similes, and analogies from all over the landscape and teaches anyone willing to listen; he carries his promise of a kingdom of love into any town and village. Indeed, he even carries it into the city that held the forces of his destruction, his beloved Jerusalem. Throughout Matthew's Gospel, we see Jesus as a man reaching out to make intimate contact with people's hearts, desperate to convert them to a happier way of living. Oddly enough, there's something of the drowning man in Jesus—it's as if he has precious little time and needs to make people notice him crying out before it's too late. In fact, the danger is that if they miss out on what he's saying, it may be too late for *them*; the miracle is that he doesn't seem to be motivated by his own neediness, but theirs.

Furthermore, in what he says, we see an overwhelming *form* of love. Jesus' message is of a loving way to live, and it has been delivered compassionately and without destructive judgment; he's realistic about people's failings and preaches complete and mutual forgiveness, which itself may be the strongest sign of love. Whenever his detractors such as the scribes and Pharisees tried forcing him to make a choice between showing mercy and condemning a "sinner," mercy always won the day. It's hard hanging around someone who radiates that much kindness, because such a person coincidentally shines a light on our inadequacies, our natural lack of charity. If we really appreciate everything Jesus said and did, the care he took to guide his listeners to a freer and more fulfilling life, and his willingness to face the hatred this aroused in people of an opposite disposition, we can feel we're in the presence of a love so hot it could burn up our souls and reduce who we have been to ashes. Of course, his intention is for us to rise phoenix-like and better. It is still a frightening idea, because we are naturally resistant to change; we fear losing ourselves—what will be left on the other side of the transformation? Maybe that's why Jesus said the kingdom of God starts out as something tiny: too much too soon would devastate us.

Not just in Matthew's Gospel, but throughout the entire New Testament, we are made aware of the terrifying idea that "God is Love," and to contemplate entering a relationship with such a force is akin to being invited into the heart of the sun: "The sun is a billion nuclear furnaces; come, be warm!" It is potentially a repulsive offer, and we must frequently be reminded of our safety, of our ability to with-stand the force of such power. "Come to me….For my yoke is easy and my burden is light" (Matt 11:28, 30) is just such a reminder. If we see Jesus as someone on fire with love, but tense because he knew he must always suppress it, in order to attract us to the flame rather than overwhelm us with its heat, we may better understand why he had pity more than anger for his persecutors; why he lashed out at hypo-critical shallowness because it deliberately puts the hypocrite outside the possibility of love; why he taught people to love and then died for them on a cross to save their souls.

An abundance of such selfless love is very hard to take. It calls on me to switch from my habitual, comfortable, and dare I say, pleasura-ble selfishness, with all its necessary but clever (and in their own way pleasurable) rationalizations, many of which I have gotten used to and which I more or less see myself enjoying for the rest of my existence, to a state where I must be bothered about other people for *their* sake, even when their sake will bring no material good in return. The thought of this is what endlessly aggravates me about Jesus' love. There's no way I can actually say I like encountering it. It's the most dis-likable—dare I say, *dangerous*—thing about him.

CHAPTER 16

WHAT WOULD JESUS' STUDENTS BE LIKE?

A while ago I said that Jesus was a great teacher, so it follows that people who read his teachings are his students. Now, not everyone who studies his teachings would necessarily agree with them or want to put them into practice. You can read many books about famous philosophers and great thinkers, many of whom wrote and spoke more words than Jesus did, and you can come to the conclusion that much of what they said was rubbish, and therefore not put their teachings into practice. It's a free world. However, suppose a student of Jesus' teachings decided to model him- or herself after him? What would that "Christian" person actually be like, assuming he or she was the genuine article and not some pretender, wearing a hypocritical Christian mask? Let's review all the teachings one more time from this angle, and try to imagine what they might produce.

First, let's recall the episode of the devil's temptation of Jesus and the desired behavior it suggests to a follower. I suppose the first thing that comes to mind is that a Christian would need to be able to deny him- or herself, and be tough in adversity. *The Hunger Games* has got nothing on forty days without bread in a desert! (Not that anyone's suggesting we should all run out, find a desert, and then starve ourselves to be like him; the main point is the *fortitude* we learn from the story.) Furthermore, the Christian would need to be serious-minded about his or her mission in life. I don't mean humorless or obsessed. I mean serious-minded; there's a difference. Jesus had a sense of humor. Anyone who can paint a picture, as he does, of a person who sees "the speck in your neighbor's eye, but [doesn't] notice the log" in their own, enjoys a delicious sense of the absurd (see Matt 7). I would certainly not want my eye surgeon to operate on me in that condition!

From the story of the temptations, we get the idea that we should follow not just the "good" but the "greater good." It's fine to be a benevolent leader of a worldly kingdom; it's better to promote a kingdom of the Spirit.

So, inner strength, serious-mindedness about a mission in life, and commitment to the greater good, which in Jesus' terms means spiritual good, are the first things we would expect to find in a committed student of Jesus who wanted to adopt the teachings and not just learn about them.

From the Beatitudes we get meekness, a hunger *and* a thirst for righteousness, a disposition to be merciful not punitive, purity of motivation, and a commitment to peace.

So the list begins to grow:

Inner strength;
Serious-mindedness;
Commitment to the greater good;
Meekness;
Strong desire for righteousness;
Mercifulness;
Motivations untinged by duplicity;
Willingness to work for peace.

Are any of these characteristics contradictory? You can be meek to the outside world and still be tough inside. You can want righteousness to prevail and still be merciful to people. It's a tightrope act, but it's possible.

The Sermon on the Mount really piles it on! Most people would agree that it's wrong to murder, but Jesus goes the full distance: anger toward another person is to be avoided as much as possible. Lustful thoughts are to be avoided as much as possible. *Wait!* What's the difference between love and lust? Shakespeare captures it best:

Love comforteth like sunshine after rain,
But lust's effect is tempest after sun;
Love's gentle spring doth always fresh remain,
Lust's winter comes ere summer half be done;
Love surfeits not, Lust like a glutton dies;
Love is all truth, Lust full of forged lies.*

One might say that lust treats another person as a sex object, something to be used without commitment; love, on the other hand, recognizes and treats the other as a whole person.

Marriage is to be respected. A vengeful form of justice ("an eye for an eye…") is to be replaced with a tolerance of the bully's venom, at least when it's you being bullied. Enemies are to be loved and prayed for. (He himself did this on the cross.) Furthermore, you have to love people who do not love you.

So, what do we add to the list?

Avoid murderous anger;
Avoid lust;
Avoid divorce;
Replace revenge with tolerance;
Love and pray for enemies and people who don't love you.

Hold on a minute—avoid lust? Avoid anger? Is it even possible? Well, no. It's not entirely possible for humans. His point, actually, is the impossibility, because he's setting up for the idea that salvation, that is, the ultimate healing of all these earthly imperfections, is only possible through the mercy of God. However there is a difference between *ultimate salvation* and *desired behavior*. We can be "saved" from spiritual annihilation, but we continue to live in this world. So what do we strive for while we are still *here*? When praying for guidance, what's our road map, and where do we want to go? This guide to living tells us that we are not hapless moral weaklings; Jesus assumes we can be

---

*William Shakespeare, *Venus and Adonis*, Line 799–804. These are the words of Adonis in the poem, *Venus and Adonis* by William Shakespeare, written in 1592–93. See http://www.bartleby.com/70/48.html.

responsible agents in this world and that we can make better choices *now*—and choices for the *better*.

So, let's look at the list again, taking onboard the additions and connecting the dots:

> Inner strength and outer meekness;
> Serious-mindedness (which doesn't mean obsession or lack of humor!);
> Commitment to the greater good, when there's a choice of "goods";
> Strong desire for righteousness;
> Avoiding murderous anger;
> Avoiding lust and having commitment to the whole other person (marriage);
> Avoiding revenge and practicing mercy, which includes loving and praying for enemies and people who don't love you; and
> Through this behavior, becoming a peacemaker.

I don't know about you, but I'm getting tired just imagining it, and we've hardly started! Also from the Sermon on the Mount, we're told that a genuine follower of Jesus would never boast about his or her own goodness, and wouldn't do any of these things for self-glorification. Therefore, selflessness, too, is a mark of the Christian. Prayer, too, would be a largely private activity, done from a desire to communicate with God rather than the intention of appearing holy. The genuine follower wouldn't hoard money ("store up for yourselves treasure in heaven…"), wouldn't be greedy, would be calm and not worry about the future very much, and would be more concerned about fixing up what's wrong with their own behavior than judging others. To summarize, the genuine follower would follow the Golden Rule and treat other people the way he or she would like to be treated.

So now the list becomes:

> Inner strength and outer meekness;
> Serious-mindedness (which doesn't mean obsession or lack of humor!);

Commitment to the greater good, when there's a choice of
    "goods";
Strong desire for righteousness;
Avoiding murderous anger;
Avoiding lust and having commitment to the whole other
    person (marriage);
Avoiding revenge and practicing mercy, which includes loving
    and praying for enemies and people who don't
    love you;
Being a peacemaker;
Being self-effacing, selfless, and not seeking personal glory;
Being privately prayerful;
Being generous, not greedy;
Staying calm and trustful;
Accepting, not being judgmental; and
Treating others the way you want to be treated.

I'm deliberately going over these lists a few times, for the sheer challenge of it all to sink in. Let's not forget that this extraordinary vision of how human beings could be as opposed to how they so often are came from one man; true, a man riding atop the Jewish tradition of justice and mercy, but still, one man. And still it isn't over!

The willing student of Jesus would reach out to the sick, the neglected, and the outcast. He or she would need to reach out even to the most hated members of the community, and socialize with them. He or she would be unafraid to break society's rules if it meant following the higher rule of compassionate love. He or she would need to be entirely nonracist, and, further, do everything he or she could do to surpass mere familial loyalty and favor other people's children to the same extent as he or she would do to his or her own. A committed student of Jesus would not easily accept rationalizations for war but would seek solutions that were right and just, because the "enemy" is part of the same spiritual family.

Now, not to labor the point, here are just these new additions to the list:

Compassion for the sick and the socially rejected;

Interest in the spiritual well-being of hated members of the community;

Being guided by compassionate behavior more than rigid social rules;

Being nonracist;

Being non-*genist*, treating equally one's own children and those of other people;

Challenging the rationalizations of wars, seeking peaceful solutions; in other words, "loving the enemy" at an international level as well as a personal one.

Of course, other characteristics reflect Jesus' behaviors as well as his teaching:

Staying compassionate even when he or she is wrung out with his or her own troubles;

Warmly welcoming children and never wishing them either physical or spiritual harm;

Staying endlessly forgiving;

Seeing leadership and power as a chance to serve others; and

Recognizing the right of his or her "neighbor" (that is, all other people) to be treated with the same care and dignity as he or she would wish to receive.

All of these attributes are an expression of the central love of God. Achieving them is a lifelong enterprise of the keen student of Jesus. It would be a year-in-year-out labor of love, with the result that the person would become more authentic in their values, more earnestly desiring of the good of others, and thus, in a sense, would become more *real*. In fact, to draw a sharp contrast, there is one thing a genuine follower of Jesus could *not* be, and that is the opposite of "real"—a hypocrite.

However, achieving such an enterprise can't be done, Jesus tells us, without the Holy Spirit; that busy guy we mentioned earlier. Human nature is too strong to be overcome by human effort alone. We can't really hope to break free of the vicious cycle without the help of some outside force. It must be a partnership. We need to keep coming back to the teaching of Jesus and his behavior as a model, and fix our desires on becoming more like him. We have to do it even when life is thoroughly against us. None of this is easy. It wasn't easy for Jesus, who paid the ultimate price for arguing against the traditional way of the world. As we set our wills to achieve the characteristics of Jesus, we also need to keep calling on the Holy Spirit—one of the aspects (or "persons") of God's character—as our source of hope, strength, guidance, and inspiration. Its greatest power in our lives comes from our believing that Jesus was resurrected as the ultimate form of hope: eternal life—life, as another Gospel writer describes it, "to the full!" The Holy Spirit reminds us of that treasure in heaven. Strangely, by ceasing to cling to the material hope of this world, we come to find peace in this world through hope in another. It's the mysterious, ultimate paradox: to lose is to gain, and to gain lastingly, and to gain completely.

From encountering Jesus in the Gospel of Matthew, we can determine not only if we like what he says, but also if we like who he is. Based on our encounter, these lists summarize how we could try to become more like Jesus.

Now, here's a question: If we were to become more like Jesus, would we like ourselves more? Would we like being a compassionate peacemaker who enjoys the enthusiasm of children and reaches out in love, wanting to serve people and bring them hope rather than fill the world with hatred? Furthermore, if more people adopted this mode of behavior—inimical as it is to the way most human affairs are conducted most of the time—would we like this *world* more? Might we see a healthier cooperation among nations, not as rivals for resources but as mutual supporters, like one family? Might we see less war? Might we see a reduction in environmental destruction, as people reduce their dependence on a glut of worldly pleasures and became more at peace with the idea of having less? Might we, in so many ways, begin to see the kingdom of heaven for real, beyond similes and metaphors and parables?

If we like Jesus so much that we begin to act on his advice, might we even end up liking the type of person we become?

EPILOGUE

I'm standing in my local park on the Saturday between Good Friday and Easter Sunday. It's traditionally called Holy Saturday; however, in some cultures it is referred to as Black Saturday. What I see before me belies that awful title, for the sun is shining, little white clouds drift by, and the scene is full of gaiety and laughter. Children play. A smart set of amateur basketball players are doing terrific shots into the hoop. It's as happy a scene as one could imagine; it's certainly *not* how most people live most of the time on the planet.

A few years back on Good Friday, in the Philippines, I walked the Stations of the Cross in Malate, a suburb of Manila, through slums. Every few hovels, we pilgrims would stop and pray at makeshift little "stations" (tiny tables with small plastic statues and/or rosary beads on top), put together with great care by people who could not afford electricity or even their own water. Later that day, I flew out and didn't get to see Black Saturday there. My wife, who is a Filipina, now recommends that we go to the "Phil" next year for Easter and be reminded of the heavy weight that culture places on Black Saturday. I see her point. I've always thought that people should at least avoid festivities until the Sunday. Black Saturday deserves pause and reflection. Easter Sunday would perhaps be more joyful—as opposed to merely happy—if we had that extra emotional journey, that sense of deprivation before deliverance.

However, the happiness around me is not without its Christian dimension. It's very hard to lament the death of Jesus when we know that his story ends with resurrection and ascension. One of the hardest things for filmmakers, so enamored of retelling the Jesus story, is to make credible the grief of his followers on Black Saturday; we find it

103

so hard to empathize because we live on the other side of the happy ending and we know what's coming.

Dorothy L. Sayers, the author of the *Lord Peter Wimsey* detective stories, among many other short stories and novels, once wrote a radio series on the passion of Jesus Christ—the week between Palm Sunday and Easter—called *The Man Born to Be King*. In the published edition, she began with an excellent introductory essay in which she pondered whether there could ever be a true Christian tragedy. There was only one, she said, *Doctor Faustus* by Christopher Marlowe. As we've seen, it's a Christian tragedy because Faustus understands completely his need for salvation and turns away from it every opportunity he is given. Despair, the rejection of the Holy Spirit, is the only Christian tragedy.

However, Sayers insisted, the story of Jesus is ultimately a happy ending for us all:

> In the fifth act….the Hero is recognised for what He is: and immediately, what was the blackest human tragedy turns into the Divine Comedy….Where Christ is, cheerfulness will keep breaking in.*

Comedy, in the original sense of life-affirming joy, always breaks through the deepest suffering because of the resurrection. "A Christian can never be alone," as a wise pope once remarked. That's our inheritance: ultimate assurance.

Joy, if based on this ultimate assurance, isn't a crime; it's virtually a Christian instinct. If we can manage to keep in mind the cost *then*, which provided the joy *now*, we can be permitted to smile, even on the blackest of Saturdays.

I like the man who made that possible.

Well that's all, folks. That's our journey in search of the likeable Jesus over—at least for now.

---

*Dorothy L Sayers, *The Man Born to Be King* (San Francisco: Ignatius Press, 1990), 20.

OH, AND…

I suppose for the sake of completeness, the last word should be Matthew's. In fact, they should be the last words from his Gospel, and after the resurrection:

> Jesus came and said to them,…"Go therefore and make disciples of all nations, baptizing them in the name of the Father and of the Son and of the Holy Spirit, and teaching them to obey everything that I have commanded you. And remember, I am with you always, to the end of the age." (Matt 28:18–20)